Moderating the Debate

Rationality and the
Promise of American Education

Moderating
the
Debate

Rationality and the
Promise of American Education

◻

MICHAEL J. FEUER

HARVARD EDUCATION PRESS
CAMBRIDGE, MASSACHUSETTS

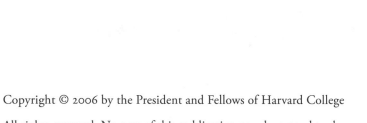

Library of Congress Control Number 2005937614

Paperback 10-digit ISBN 1-891792-69-5
Library Edition 10-digit ISBN 1-891792-70-9

Paperback 13-digit ISBN 978-1-891792-69-4
Library Edition 13-digit ISBN 978-1-891792-70-0

Published by Harvard Education Press,
an imprint of the Harvard Education Publishing Group

Harvard Education Press
8 Story Street
Cambridge, MA 02138

Cover Design: Alyssa Morris

The typeface used in this book is Adobe Garamond Pro. Designed
by Robert Slimbach, Adobe Garamond is a digital interpretation of
the roman types of Claude Garamond and the italic types of Robert
Granjon. With the introduction of OpenType font technology, Adobe
Garamond has been reissued as a "Pro" type family that takes advantage
of OpenType's advanced typographic capabilities.

08/26/08

To the memory of Otto and Lucy Feuer,

Who knew to be wise and practical

And to my family,

Regine, Sarah, Jonathan,

For whom my love is rationally unbounded

Contents

Preface

Students of the history of American education are accustomed to drama. Reports of the condition of our schools are usually laced with large doses of gloom and doom, proposals for reform typically promise extraordinary solutions timed to coincide neatly with electoral cycles; we are always at the edge of economic and social ruin, about to be overrun by international rivals with superior schools and smarter students. But the rhetoric of reform promises salvation. In recent years, at least since the 1983 publication of "A Nation at Risk," perhaps the most influential government-sponsored report ever on matters of public education, the trend toward exuberance has only worsened—or become more comical, depending on one's perspective. Our first effort to establish national educational goals, for example, included the promise that the United States would be "number 1 in the world in science and mathematics by the year 2000," a rather unrealistic vision that prompted one wag to suggest there had been a typographical error and that we might reach the goal in 2,000 years. More recently, the landmark 2001 No Child Left Behind Act, notable for its bipartisan support and bold insistence on high standards for all children, also made some rather ambitious promises: the idea that all students in America would reach "proficiency" by 2014 flies in the face of nearly all empirical evidence on the capability of the system to change at the implied pace.

Why education in our democracy seems so vulnerable to political hyperbole is a question that many distinguished scholars have addressed. As the eminent historian Lawrence Cremin noted in *Popular Education and Its Discontents,* the last book before his untimely death, education is political because it symbolizes the Aristotelian ethic to pursue "the good life," and in democracies where people are encouraged both to seek personal improvement and to govern their own schools, decisions about education inevitably ignite a shrill ideological cacophony. As political history goes, this explanation is helpful. Indeed, it is foolish to seek understanding of our current education debates without a solid grasp of their political, cultural, and historical contexts.

The awareness that education is political, however, and that education politics is especially noisy, still begs some important questions. Why, for example, does the principle of political compromise, so fundamental to democratic society, seem to elude the rhetoric of school reform? Why do Americans, famous for pragmatism, tolerate ambiguity and incremental progress in many areas but seem mesmerized by a fantasy of quick fixes when it comes to the education of their children? Is there a psychology that explains the preference for dramatic pronouncements, grandiose proposals, and the inevitable cycle of euphoria and disappointment? What would it take to lower the heat on the rhetoric of educational change, establish reasonable standards of research evidence to guide reform proposals, and come to agreement about realistic strategies with reasonable timetables? *What would a rational approach to education policy look like?*

In the raucous intersection of science and politics where I have worked for close to 25 years, I often ponder these questions, especially as my work brings me in close contact with the education research and policy communities. Trained in policy analysis and biased toward models that bridge economics, organization theory, and psychology, I have often wondered if the so-called cognitive revolution, the study of human decisionmaking and rational judgment, could help explain the apparent nonrationality of education policy and discourse. So, when my friend Ellen Lagemann, then dean of the Harvard Graduate School of Education, invited me to give a series of lectures at Harvard—on a topic of my own choosing—I leapt at the chance to bring some order to my inchoate reasoning about the rationality of education.

This book is a revised and consolidated version of my Burton and Inglis Lectures, which I delivered at the Harvard Graduate School of Education during the 2004–05 academic year. Whether the fact that I have been strongly influenced by the last Burton and Inglis lecturer, Lawrence Cremin, is pure coincidence, I shall leave to the statisticians and astrologers to sort out; meanwhile, it gives me great joy mingled with a good bit of trepidation to be associated with this giant of education scholarship. My gratitude to Ellen is enormous.

The umbrella title for my lectures was "The Science of Rationality and the Rationality of Science." Unwieldy for sure, but as a first stab at what interested me it came close: what can cognitive science tell us about rational education policy? My argument focused on a mysterious gap in applied social science. Cognitive psychology, and in particular the strand focused on human information processing and decisionmaking, has been central to modern theories of teaching and learning. Indeed, many of the interesting reforms in the teaching of reading, mathematics, history, and, most recently, science are motivated in large part by research on how people integrate new information with their prior knowledge, apply formal and informal thought to solving complex problems, and mix learning and memory with discovery and invention.

The cognitive revolution has also been instrumental in shaping new theories of economic organization and public policy. Conventional economic theory that assumes human omniscience in the pursuit of self-interest has been supplanted, at least in part, by theories that take into account cognitive limits to human problem solving and the effects of social organization on the solution of complex problems. Economists today no longer approach major policy questions such as antitrust, regulation, or the environment without at least some attention to the nature of information required for rational thought and the effects of organizational arrangements on economic outcomes. It is something of a mystery, therefore, that the cognitive revolution has barely touched education policy and the organization of schooling. There seems to be a missing link in the evolution of cognitive science: *theories of rational thought have influenced education and have influenced policy—but have skated over* education policy.

Exploring this puzzle and attempting to find the missing pieces are the themes of this book. My approach builds on the notion of *procedural rationality,* a term coined by the Nobel laureate Herbert Simon to describe the process people use to search for reasonably good solutions—rather than "best" ones—when faced with truly complex problems. My analysis of cognitive research and its applications, and my review of the political and cultural context of education in the United States, leads to a procedurally rational strategy for sustainable education reform. The bottom line, if that is the right imagery for a book such as this, is that the rational approach to solving our toughest education problems is to look for better—and not necessarily best—results.

I have benefited greatly from the comments of many colleagues and friends. Bruce Alberts, immediate past president of the National Academy of Sciences, has been a staunch supporter of bringing scientific research to bear on education policy and enthusiastically encouraged me to pursue this project. I am grateful also to Bill Colglazier, executive officer at the Academies, for his kind encouragement. Many of my colleagues at the Academies have heard me talk about this project, and I thank them for their indulgence. It is important to note, however, that neither the Academies nor any of its constituent boards or committees necessarily share the opinions and recommendations in this book, for which I take sole responsibility.

Mike McPherson, a relatively new friend who now heads The Spencer Foundation, read all three lectures and reacted with wise and provocative ideas; some of his wisdom has seeped into these pages, and more of it will influence future work. Dick Murnane, a colleague, mentor, and friend for now close to 30 years, came to the lectures, provided much needed moral support, and offered his characteristic insights, especially on chapter 3. Catherine Snow and Nonie Lessaux, discussants at two of the lectures, patiently showed me how their own specialties could inform my thinking. I thank also the other discussants, Jennifer Steele, Michael Connell, Vanessa Fong, Susan Moore Johnson, Mica Pollack, and Kathleen Guiney. Richard Atkinson read all three papers and with his inimitable appreciation for the connections between science and policy encouraged me in fundamental ways. Lee Shulman has been a wonderfully supportive friend, and I am grateful for the wisdom of his practice and the practice of his wisdom. Mike Smith reads everything I send him and always tells me quickly and clearly what he thinks. Bettie St. Pierre alerted me to basic epistemological issues relating to scientific inquiry and attempted to steer me clear of postmodern thickets. Ernie House, an evaluation methodologist who has wandered quite successfully into the territory usually reserved for economists, provided very useful comments. My very dear friend Bob Linn read the papers and checked my reasoning, especially on matters concerning assessment and accountability. Bob Hauser, Dan Koretz, Nancy Cartwright, Andrew Morris, Fernando Reimers, Larry Suter, and Barbara Torrey all offered useful suggestions. Lisa Towne, former student and now colleague par excellence, brought me back on course when I roamed from the facts of the education research debates. Avital Darmon, who is largely responsible for a fabulously interesting experiment in education research and policy in Israel, read all three papers and reacted thoughtfully and quickly. Avital also helped arrange an opportunity for me to present thoughts in progress to faculty and students at Hebrew University of Jerusalem, and I wish to thank Eran Feitelson and his colleagues in the public-policy program for their hospitality and thoughtful reactions. My daughter, Sarah Feuer, a budding historian and loving critic, gave me especially helpful comments on tone and helped me understand how my ideas on rationality would be heard.

Finally, I wish to acknowledge a number of individuals who have made it possible for me to turn my ideas into lectures, my lectures into papers, and the papers now into this book. Shawn Tuttle of the Harvard education school handled all the logistics of my visits to Cambridge with grace, wit, and efficiency. Chris McShane, one of the best editors at the National Research Council, helped me with everything from citations to subtitles. Doug Clayton, Caroline Chauncey, and Dody Riggs, my editors at Harvard Education Press, were absolutely superb at all stages, and Jeff Perkins was a skillful advisor on marketing strategies. We were also greatly helped by the expert copy editing of Daniel Simon.

I t is customary in academic circles to end a long list of acknowledgments with the reminder that those listed are not responsible for remaining errors. I will not attempt to break that tradition, but I will just add again how grateful I am to all these people—and to Ellen and the Harvard community, especially—for their abiding friendship and support.

Michael J. Feuer
Washington, D.C.
November 2005

INTRODUCTION

◉

What Is Rationality?

When the rabbi of a poor town won the lottery, his community gathered to celebrate its new wealth.

"How did you know to pick number 42?" asked an awe-struck young disciple.

"I dreamed I saw 7 brides dancing with 7 grooms, so I multiplied them together and got 42," answered the rabbi, scratching his beard as though in deep thought.

"But rabbi," shot back the young student, "with all respect, 7 x 7 is 49, not 42."

"Oh? Okay, so *you* be the mathematician."

Yiddish folktale

Years ago I had a good friend (let's call him R) who developed a mathematical model of options trading, a specialty of the 1980s stock market, which should have made him a rich man. R was a mathematical prodigy and attracted to games of skill and chance. He played competitive chess and bridge, and enjoyed counting cards and trying to beat the house at blackjack. His options model was the product of many years of work, and an example of his intellectual elegance. One only had to enter some readily available data about the market and about one's own "position," and the algorithm would yield the equivalent of buy and sell instructions. Each transaction would not necessarily result in financial gain, but over time the average performance of the model would be substantially better than chance: in other words, the model could beat the odds. Using historical data, R demonstrated retrospectively—to himself and potential investors—that by following his model's rules they could win big.

What went wrong? Unfortunately, R *knew too much* about the workings of the market. Of course, without that knowledge he would not have been able (or motivated) to construct the model in the first place. But too often his knowledge prevented him from doing the right thing, from following his own model's results. For instance, if the model said "sell," R would typically look at his position, look at other market data, recall similar situations, and he would think. These were instinctive responses of an analytical and deliberative mind. Too often, though, R became convinced there was an error *in the model,* so he would override its recommended course of action and rely instead on his own intuitive judgment. That intuition, born of formal knowledge, experience, recognition of patterns, and what might best be called strong hunches, led him to veto the mathematically and objectively correct—albeit unbelievable—decision rule. I remember asking R why he didn't automate the system and let the model communicate directly with a floor trader without his personal intervention. For reasons having to do with market regulations, I believe, that option was not available. Anyway, I doubt R would have been willing to relinquish control of the decisions, precisely because he believed in his own intuitive judgments.

We didn't discuss this at the time, but in retrospect I believe R was guided, perhaps subconsciously, by his beliefs about personal control and the dignity of human volition in an increasingly technological world. In any case, the irony in this story is rich. At his day job, R was an accomplished clinical psychologist with a Ph.D. from a top-ranked research university. He specialized in cognitive therapy, a system oriented toward helping patients overcome thinking errors that interfered with effective personal behavior.[1] He was an empathic and supportive friend, traits that he brought into his clinic. He was also deeply self aware and sensed that something was not right in his relationship with his options model. (He loved her, but he wouldn't listen to her . . .) Sadly, or perhaps happily—depending on one's beliefs about the nature of human choice—all the cognitive massaging in the world couldn't get R to overcome the force of his own intuitive judgments. And it surely didn't help that there were times when his hunches paid off—at least in the short term: sometimes, by resisting his model's temptations, R actually *improved* his market position, which of course reinforced his determination to "think" and discouraged him from automating the whole process. But in the long run, which in fact was sadly rather short, R lost the tug-of-war between intuition and objectivity, lost much of his money, and quit the options business. He returned to the perhaps more rational world of clinical psychology, where his own personal experiences enriched his store of recognizable patterns and strengthened his hand in helping patients confront their own cognitive limitations.

It would be tempting to infer from this story that intuition should not be trusted, that heuristics should be displaced by formal models that seek objectively correct solutions, and that we would be better off ceding control of difficult problems to airtight mathematical algorithms. Surely that approach comports with my bias toward social science and analytical reasoning—but it would oversimplify a more interesting and subtle story. For there are many examples in which formal reasoning alone is clearly *not* the winning strategy.

Consider that staple of operations research, economics, and information science, the "traveling-salesman problem" (TSP): *given a finite number of cities along with the cost of traveling between each pair of them, find the cheapest way of visiting all the cities and returning to your starting point.*[2] I have often borrowed this example and embellished it for dramatic effect in my policy courses and in some lectures, and it usually evokes just the desired kind of "ah-ha" response. It seems like a logical and simple assignment: list all possible routes, calculate the mileage for each one, then scan the list for the route with lowest cost.

Logical, yes. But simple? If you think so, then take a few minutes to figure out how many combinations of routes there would be for a small case of, say, 15 cities. Those with some training in mathematical statistics know the answer: there are 15! routes (! is mathematical notation for "factorial," which means multiplying each number by its preceding number, i.e., 15 x 14 x 13 x 12 . . .), and listing all 1.3 trillion of them—1,307,674,368,000 to be precise—would take more than a few minutes. In fact, *assuming a half-minute of writing time per route, it would take about 650 billion minutes, or about 1.2 million years just to write down the complete list!* Scanning the list and then checking for errors would take, well . . . I think I have made my point. Suddenly what began as an utterly rational approach to solving a well-defined problem, one for which all the relevant data are in hand, has exploded into a combinatorial nightmare.

The moral of the story is obvious: while the salesman inclined toward mathematically optimal solutions starts compiling his list, a "less rational" competitor leaves for Syracuse and on his way decides that his next stop will be Buffalo, then remembers they had been building a new route to Utica the last time he was in the area, and so on. *In the time it takes the rationalist to write down maybe a millionth of 1 percent of the possible routes, Mr. Seat-of-the-Pants visits all 15 cities and makes it back home in time for Thanksgiving.* Granted, he will not have necessarily *minimized* cost, and so in a way he has violated the principal goal of the exercise; but his losses are more than compensated by the capture of the bedeviled rationalist's erstwhile customers.

It is worth taking a moment to think about the key elements of the TSP and why it frequently shows up as a metaphor in theories of rationality, organization, and decisionmaking. First, it should be intuitively clear that at least one optimum exists for any standard TSP; indeed, there may be several routes that minimize cost, but there must always be at least one, in the same way that any list of numbers has at least one that is the smallest. Thus, the idea of searching for an optimum is not, prima facie, a silly one; the challenge, rather, is in the implementation—that is, in conducting a *computationally feasible* search.[3]

Second, the idea that people would *want* to find the optimum is also not far-fetched. Cost-*minimization,* profit-*maximization,* and utility-*maximization* are core assumptions of economic theory largely because they reflect a plausible and even laudable aspiration. The assumption that people wish to behave efficiently is both salutary and realistic, even if their capacity is severely constrained.[4]

Third, probably the most interesting part of the TSP is not so much the right answer but rather the realization that searching for it is not necessarily the smart thing to do, given the limits on human information processing or, as Herbert Simon called it, our *bounded rationality.*[5] There is a subtle but significant divergence between human intent—the desire to behave rationally—and the cognitive limits we face in solving complex problems. In the case of the TSP, the presence of competition and the desire to maintain one's customers means that truly rational thought would take account of context: most importantly, the cost of computation measured in terms of time and the economic opportunities forgone during that time.[6]

Finally, the TSP has become a trivial exercise except perhaps for cases with an extremely large number of cities, thanks to the increased speed and capacity of electronic computing.[7] (Still, it is not obvious that the average traveling salesman would have access to the kind of computer needed to solve the routing problem; one suspects that if he did he might not be a salesman in the first place!) As metaphor, however, it remains powerful: rationality is situation-dependent, involves a blend of formal computation and heuristic judgment depending on the complexity of the problem and the availability of technology, and is the result of *appropriate* rather than exhaustive deliberation. This lies at the core of Herbert Simon's exquisite insight that *substantively rational thought,* or the pursuit of optimal answers, may not be *procedurally* rational.[8]

That rational judgment is bounded by cognitive limits, that complex problems are not necessarily solvable solely by objective (as opposed to intuitive or subjective) thought, and that intuition in appropriate doses is a necessary ingredient of rational decisionmaking have been familiar ideas to psychologists and philosophers for a long time.[9] Nonetheless, new models of rational thought (associated with the contributions of Simon and his colleagues) have shaken the foundations of economic, political, and organization theory, challenged so-called positivist theories of science, and significantly enriched emerging models of policy analysis that would otherwise rest on different (and implausible) assumptions about how humans solve complex problems.[10] Simon may have been a tad optimistic when he wrote that "procedural rationality will become one of the central concerns of economics over the next 25 years,"[11] but there is little argument that his challenge to conventional theory led the way to behavioral economics, injected new life into organization theory, and resuscitated interest in comparative institutions and the governance of economic and social transactions.[12]

Somewhat paradoxically, however, education policy—including theories of school organization and reform as well as strategies for relevant and useful education research—have not benefited much from this cognitively inspired revolution. This is surprising, because today's mainstream theories of teaching, learning, human performance, and assessment can be traced to advances in cognitive science generally and to Simon's work specifically. Herein lies a mystery: *The science of rationality has made a profound mark on the understanding of human teaching and learning, but has been largely ignored in the pursuit of rational strategies for school improvement and education research.*[13]

In this book I offer an approach to replacing the missing link, and argue for importing lessons of cognitive psychology to the theory and practice of education policy. My optimism over the potential for a cognitively inspired strategy stems from three sources: (1) the extraordinary success of the cognitive revolution as a tool for understanding human learning; (2) the success, less extraordinary but nevertheless significant, of cognitive science as the foundation for an organization theory applied to such policy domains as antitrust law, labor markets, hospital management, and the theory of the firm; and (3) my experience in the real world of education policy, where decades of well-intentioned but unrealistic goals suggest the need for a new model of rationality.

I begin in chapter 1 by reviewing selectively the contributions of cognitive science to theories of human performance, learning, and assessment. Then I describe some developments in organization theory and policy analysis—in domains other than education—that derive from the cognitive view of rational decisionmaking.

In chapter 2 I take a fresh look at major education policy and reform efforts of the latter half of the twentieth century through the cognitive-organizational lens. The focus is on organizational complexities (environmental conditions) and the implicit cognitive demands these complexities impose on educators and policymakers. This view reflects the underlying proposition that rational decisionmaking is a function both of the mental and technological resources available for computation and of the objective complexity implicit in the decisionmaking problem. With this analysis I hope to make the case that education policy—including the currently hot debate over standards of evidence, methodology, and the funding of user-oriented research—would be fertile ground for a cognitively inspired theory: that is, one that applies principles of cognitive science and procedural rationality to the development of reasonable and realistic school reform strategies.

In chapter 3 I lay out a modest proposal for improved mutual understanding between researchers and policymakers, respect for appropriate deliberation as the basis for program design, and the development of *reasonable* rather than *optimal* goals for education reform and the improvement of schooling.

CHAPTER I

◼

Cognitive Science, Learning, and Organization

> Optimization does not necessarily constitute the optimal approach to decision making.
> *William J. Baumol, "On Rational Satisficing," 2004*

Psychological science has come a long way since the days of Freud and Skinner. We now appreciate that neither toilet training nor conditioned response are sufficient to explain the complex and amazing phenomena called thought and behavior. Thanks to decades of scientific advancement, we now have a rich research literature on how the mind works, how it is connected to thought, and how thought relates to behavior; much of all this is the result of psychobiological interactions deep inside our gray matter. Welcome to cognitive science.[1]

I am mostly interested in the strands of this research that I can make relevant to education policy and organization, and I will therefore emphasize findings and conclusions that seem traceable to what might be called the Simon school of learning as problem solving.[2] It is perhaps best to start with reference to a great tectonic shift that shook the foundations of psychology starting in the late 1940s. Ellen Lagemann summarizes this critical passage from "behaviorism" to "cognitivism" in her history of education research,[3] and Howard Gardner has written a rich and nuanced biography of the life of cognitive science,[4] so it is not necessary here to digress into all the details. But some key elements of what Gardner called the "cognitive revolution" are especially relevant to my problem-solving concerns in this book.

Behaviorism was an approach to studying the human mind that emphasized inputs (stimuli) and outputs (thought, action). It was more concerned with those observables (and their proxy measures) than with the intricacies of brain functioning "inside the black box." In that sense, behaviorism coincided with the ascendance of positivism in social science. In neoclassical economics, for example, the dominant epistemology has favored prediction of outcomes based on assumed efficiency in the conversion of inputs, without much interest in *how* the conversion actually takes place.[5]

The emergence of electronic computing captivated the attention not only of mathematicians interested in computation but, as importantly, the interests of psychologists, linguists, and organization theorists who sensed the opportunity to look inside that famous black box and discover how humans convert stimuli into rational thought and behavior. As Lagemann notes, "Innovations [in computing technology] allowed mathematicians, psychologists, and others to begin investigating cognition through analogy rather than through observation and presumed correlations between selected stimuli and behavior."[6]

If one of the advantages of behaviorism was its parsimony—measuring observable stimuli and outcomes was technically more feasible than exploring the complex inner workings of the human mind—high-speed computing technology offered a viable alternative. The convergence of computer science and cognitive theory is one of the more stunning examples of how scientific thought and technological development have at critical times been mutually dependent: the brains behind early computer technology (John von Neumann, J. A. Brainerd, Alan Newell, Norbert Wiener, and others) were obviously influenced by their own ideas about how the human mind worked, while scholars who were primarily interested in human cognition learned much from the results of experiments with those early computers.

In retrospect, one might say that the science of the mind was becoming procedurally rational as a research strategy owing in large part to the accomplishments of mathematicians and computer scientists like von Neumann, who developed MANIAC, the first "giant electronic brain"; and Brainerd of the University of Pennsylvania, who was one of the leaders in the development of ENIAC, the first electronic numerical integrator and computer.[7]

The simultaneity and mutual dependence of psychological theory and computing technology became apparent when scholars working in these diverse fields came together, for example, at the Hixon Symposium at Cal Tech in 1948 and in subsequent seminars throughout the late 1950s and 1960s; figuring out which came first, von Neumann's computer or Karl Lashley's revolt against behaviorism, is perhaps an interesting academic chicken-and-egg problem, but I would argue not as important as recognizing how the simultaneity influenced (and was influenced by) the thought and work of people like George Miller, Ulric Neisser, and Herbert Simon, as well as the development of the science of cognition.[8]

If one were to summarize the principal assumptions and strategies of cognitive theory, especially the "information processing" strand most relevant to the work of Simon and others (and therefore to my agenda in this book), the list would be likely to include two key items. First, we would find an emphasis on microlevel mental tasks involved in solving problems, by which I mean the workings of the mind in converting stimuli (both internal and external), rather than the behaviorist approach, which settles for measurement of the observable products of that conversion.[9] In other words, the issue of interest is the actual processes—and not only the results—of cognitive activity. Second, the list would include the principle of computational feasibility—how much data can the mind process?—in defining rational cognitive functioning. Here the important insight is that practical limitations matter: it is simply not realistic to expect rational thinkers to possess capacities for computation that are biologically unlikely or otherwise infeasible.

Gardner's rich history of cognitive psychology captured the essence of the information-processing, or problem-solving, model. As he notes, the cognitive revolution yielded a more dynamic view of problem-solving, including informational access mechanisms, retention and memory, and "higher-order control mechanisms whose mission it is to determine which problems ought to be tackled, which goals sought, which operations applied, and in which order."[10]

FROM COGNITION TO LEARNING

How did these fundamentals of cognitive theory reshape learning theory? Again, a complete mapping of this evolution would be impossible in this space, so I shall push my pins in at places most relevant to my effort to import lessons from psychological theory to education policy. A good place to begin is with Lauren Resnick's 1987 monograph *Education and Learning to Think* (perhaps especially interesting because, in addition to laying out an agenda for the reform of teaching, it summarized Resnick's own transition from her early behaviorist roots into a standard-bearer for the cognitive revolution).[11] Her model connected basic notions of cognition to evolving principles for education. The most important single message of research on how people acquire the skill and propensity for thought is that the kinds of activities traditionally associated with thinking are not limited to advanced levels of development. Rather, they are an intimate part of even elementary levels of reading, mathematics, and other branches of learning.

The term *higher-order skills* is misleading, therefore, because it suggests that mastery of another set of *lower*-order skills needs to come first. This assumption—that there is a hierarchical sequence of mental activities, from low-level ones that do not require much independent thinking or judgment to higher-level ones that do—colored much education theory and practice. Among education researchers who know their history, the name Edward Thorndike evokes images of teaching as the unzipping of children's heads and the pouring in of sufficient quantities of atomized bits of information in the hope they would eventually build up to a capacity for creative thought.[12] Cognitive research, especially in the hands of enlightened thinkers like Resnick, reworked our understanding of the nature of such skills as reading and mathematics and provided a rigorous antidote to the mechanized behaviorism of Thorndike and others. Learners cannot understand what they read without making inferences and using information (from other sources, from prior experience, from intuition) that goes beyond what is written in the text. They cannot become good writers without engaging in complex problem-solving processes. Basic mathematics cannot be learned effectively if learners try only to memorize rules for manipulating the numerical symbols.

But are these capacities innate? Not according to Resnick et al. Rather, many components of higher-order thinking can be effectively taught, including problem solving in specific disciplines as well as general problem-solving skills, reading and study strategies, self-monitoring skills, special training to improve general intelligence, and teaching general reasoning and argumentation skills. However, lest we become too optimistic, training in the components of higher-order reasoning does not necessarily add up either to an integrated ability to learn, think, and reason or to a broad disposition to engage in higher-order thinking. Such a broad disposition must be cultivated—to know when strategies or techniques for problem solving and learning are appropriate. It also requires the motivation to apply them, even though they may involve more effort than routine performance and some risk of social controversy.

Resnick's monograph summarized findings from the emergent cognitive approach to learning theory,[13] and it came at a time of renewed public and political interest in school reform.[14] In the decade that followed, cognitive research applied to teaching and learning continued apace, and in some ways produced ideas that were too demanding (cognitively and otherwise) for the world of policy and practice.[15]

It was in this period, for example, that researchers noticed how new theories of learning were not accompanied by new models of assessment, which of course led to a fundamental predicament: new learning theory could not be fairly evaluated with a psychometrics that had been designed for behaviorist principles, but a new psychometrics would be slow in developing and vulnerable to an array of challenges to its validity and reliability.[16] Put differently, the cognitive revolution encountered a fundamental paradox. To be scientific, the theory needed a valid system of measurement; available measures of mental functioning were aligned to behaviorist theories and would therefore provide incomplete (or erroneous) indications of learning; new measures more appropriate to emerging theory would take time to develop and, more critically, would not enable tests of the new theory against the one it was displacing. How would we know if a cognitive theory is better than a behaviorist theory at explaining mental processes if we don't use a measurement tool valid for both? By comparison, imagine the emergence of a new theory of economic development that could not be adequately assessed using available economic metrics. How would policymakers be able to judge the validity of the proposed alternative to conventional thinking?

This was also the era of exciting new work on the differences between novices and experts, with implications for training; the development of theories of practical intelligence and multiple intelligences; increasingly strident debates over situated versus transferable intelligence; and the development of important new theories of knowledge representation and measurement.[17]

By 1998 there was enough activity—and, of course, controversy—to justify a synthesis and stock-taking by the National Research Council. Two committees were charged with critical reviews of the field, the first concentrating on learning theory and the sequel on assessment. In retrospect, the logic was consistent with the assessment paradox mentioned earlier: evaluating and implementing the advantages of cognitive theory for the practice of teaching and learning would necessitate the design of a new and more relevant psychometrics. The National Research Council syntheses are worth summarizing.

How People Learn

In the early part of the twentieth century, education focused on the acquisition of basic literacy skills: simple reading, writing, and calculating.[18] Schools were not expected to train people to think and read critically, to express themselves clearly and persuasively, or to solve complex problems in science and mathematics. But with cognitive research came a new theory of learning with major implications for the design of curriculum, teaching, and assessment.

Cognitive development is not merely biological but is also an active process that derives essential information from experience. The functional organization of the brain and the mind depends on and benefits positively from experience. Research has shown that some experiences have the most powerful effects during specific sensitive periods, while others can affect the brain over a much longer time span.

One of the hallmarks of this new theory of learning is its emphasis on *learning with understanding*. Usable knowledge is not the same as a list of disconnected facts. Research on expertise in such areas as chess, history, science, and mathematics demonstrates that experts have acquired extensive knowledge that affects what they notice and how they organize, represent, and interpret information in their environment, which in turn affects their abilities to remember, reason, and solve problems.

Experts are more likely than novices to recognize meaningful patterns of information, whether on a chessboard or a circuit board. They seek to understand problems by thinking in terms of core concepts or "big ideas," such as Newtonian principles underlying physics problems or the big picture of a historical era. Experts have not only acquired knowledge but are also good at retrieving the knowledge that is relevant to a particular task. Their ability to retrieve relevant knowledge can be relatively effortless, and this fluency places fewer demands on conscious attention (think of the process of learning to drive a car). Flexibility and adaptability are found in different measure in different types of experts, and the ability to monitor one's approach to problem solving—to be metacognitive—is an important aspect of an expert's competence.

Several critical features of learning affect people's abilities to transfer what they have learned. For example, the amount and kind of initial learning is a key determinant of the development of expertise and the ability to transfer knowledge. Students are motivated to spend the time needed to learn complex subjects and to solve problems that they find interesting. Opportunities to use knowledge to create products and benefits for others are particularly motivating for students. The context in which one learns is important for promoting transfer.[19] Knowledge that is taught in only a single context is less likely to support flexible transfer than knowledge that is taught in multiple contexts. With exposure to multiple contexts, therefore, students are more likely to abstract the relevant features of concepts and develop a more flexible representation of knowledge. The use of well-chosen contrasting cases (linear and nonlinear functions, recognition memory and recall) can help students learn the conditions under which new knowledge is applicable.

Abstract representations of problems can also facilitate transfer, which is best viewed as an active, dynamic process rather than a passive end product of a particular set of learning experiences. It should require learners to actively choose and evaluate strategies, consider resources, and receive feedback. All new learning involves transfer based on previous learning, and this fact has important implications for the design of instruction that helps students learn.

History. For expert history teachers, their knowledge of the discipline and beliefs about its structure interact with their teaching strategies. Rather than simply introduce students to sets of facts to be learned, these teachers help people to understand the problematic nature of historical interpretation and analysis and to appreciate the relevance of history for their everyday lives. One teacher, noting that historians are cursed with an abundance of data that threatens to overwhelm, has his ninth-grade students create a time capsule of the most important facts from the past. Another high-school teacher thrusts her students into the kinds of epistemological issues that one might find in a graduate seminar: What is history? How do we know the past? Yet another teacher sets up her students to debate the legitimacy of British taxation in the American colonies.

Mathematics. Most people think mathematics is all about computation, but effective mathematics teachers see computation as merely a tool in the real stuff of mathematics, which includes problem solving and characterizing and understanding structure and patterns. One teacher teaches fourth graders multiplication with a set of lessons using coin problems, then simple stories and drawings, and finally numbers and symbols—a far cry from "multiplication facts."

Another takes into account children's thinking when she considers a wealth of possible models for presenting negative numbers to them: magic peanuts, money, game scoring, a frog on a number line, buildings with floors above and below ground. Another teacher's instructional practices encourage first and second graders to discuss alternative strategies to solving problems, extending to such everyday activities as sharing snacks, lunch count, and attendance.

Science. Teaching and learning in science have been influenced very directly by research on expertise. Several teaching strategies help students think about the general principles or big ideas in physics before jumping to formulas and equations. Others illustrate ways to help students engage in deliberate practice and to monitor their progress. Learning the strategies for scientific thinking has another objective: to develop thinking acumen needed to promote conceptual change. Often the barrier to achieving insights to new solutions is rooted in a fundamental misconception about the subject matter. One strategy for helping students in physics begins with an "anchoring intuition" about a phenomenon and then gradually bridges it to related phenomena that are less intuitive to the student but involve the same physics principles. Another strategy involves the use of interactive lecture demonstrations to encourage students to make predictions, consider feedback, and then reconceptualize phenomena.[20]

How We Know What People Learn

How could these enticing theories be tested if the only available measures of student learning were proxies for a discredited behaviorist conception of thought? On the other hand, how could the merits of new learning strategies be evaluated in comparison to older strategies if the traditional measures used to gauge learning were dismissed? This was the nub of the problem posed to a second NRC committee, which saw its charge as nothing less than to synthesize developments in measurement theory with the new cognitively inspired theories of teaching and learning.[21]

Contemporary theories of learning and knowing emphasize the way knowledge is represented, organized, and processed in the mind. Emphasis is also placed on the organizational dimensions of learning, including social and participatory practices that support knowing and understanding. These theories suggest that assessment practices need to move beyond component skills and discrete bits of knowledge to encompass more complex aspects of student achievement. Advances in the sciences of thinking and learning touch on the way experts organize knowledge, the importance of reflecting on and monitoring one's own thinking ("metacognition"), the transformation of naïve understanding into more complete and accurate comprehension, the usefulness of practice and feedback, and the context in which information is presented.

An important proposition underlying the new approach to assessment, which draws on principles of cognition, is that students learn more if instruction and assessment are integrally related. Good assessments can make a difference in the classroom by providing a dynamic view of students' understanding as they make their way from novice to competent performer. Large-scale assessments can benefit learning, but to derive real benefits from the merger of cognitive and measurement theory in large-scale assessment, new ways are needed for covering a broad range of competencies and capturing rich information about the nature of student understanding.

The NRC committee attempted to capture these emerging theoretical developments by proposing an "assessment triangle": all assessments consist of (1) a model of how students represent knowledge and develop competence in the subject domain, (2) tasks or situations that enable the observation of students' performance, and (3) an interpretation method for drawing inferences from the performance evidence obtained. The committee found that most widely used assessments of academic achievement, especially those most familiarly known for their standardized, short-answer, multiple-choice formats, are based on restrictive beliefs about learning and competence not consistent with current knowledge about human cognition and learning. Likewise, the elements of observation and interpretation underlying most current assessments were created to fit prior conceptions of learning and would need to be modified, according to the report, to support the kinds of inferences people now want to draw about student achievement.

Several formidable obstacles stand in the way of rapid development and acceptance of such an approach. On the technical level, advances in high-speed computing theoretically enable multidimensional representations of learning, but the software needed for such a project is still at a fairly rudimentary stage. On the practical level, the fundamental time and cost advantages of existing tests cannot be overestimated. And on the political or policy level, so long as the question about whether assessments are intended primarily to guide instruction or to provide reliable indicators of progress for public accountability purposes remains murky, the advantages of assessments that offer deeper cognitive representations will be uncertain until those representations are translated into easily understood outcome measures.

Some hope for crossing this divide and revolutionizing testing as we know it lies in the development of advanced statistical methods. The committee noted with optimism that advances in statistical methodology now make it possible to characterize student achievement in terms of multiple aspects of proficiency rather than a single score; to chart their progress over time instead of measuring performance at a particular point in time; to deal with multiple paths or alternative methods of valued performance; to model, monitor, and improve judgments on the basis of informed evaluations; and to model the performance not only of students but also of groups, classes, schools, and states. Nevertheless, many of the newer models and methods are not widely used because they are not easily understood or packaged to be accessible to those without a strong technical background.

Just as we have seen that the advent of high-speed computational technology was essential in the evolution of psychological science from behaviorism to cognitivism, new information technologies are now helping to remove some of the constraints that have limited assessment practices in the past. Testing no longer need be confined to paper-and-pencil formats, and the entire burden of classroom assessment no longer need fall on the teacher. New capabilities enabled by technology include directly assessing problem-solving skills, making visible sequences of actions taken by learners in solving problems, and modeling and simulating complex reasoning tasks.

FROM COGNITION TO ORGANIZATION

The preceding discussion has emphasized—and celebrated—connections between theories of human cognition and theories of educational development and measurement. I turn now away from education to make a different argument: namely, that cognitive theory, and in particular the strand which emphasizes decisionmaking under constraints of bounded rationality and environmental complexity, has led to a reconceptualization of assumptions and predictions in a number of public-policy domains, but almost entirely in areas other than schools and schooling. Here again, it would be unwieldy to attempt a comprehensive review of the literature on organization theory and institutional economics that has blossomed in the past half century, or a review of the myriad policy areas to which that literature has addressed itself. My selections are chosen to spur renewed interest in this line of scholarship in the context of education policy and research.

My starting point is the "organizational failures framework," proposed originally by Oliver Williamson in the early 1970s as the foundation for his revival of institutional economics.[22] A basic question posed in this work is why certain economic activities are organized as markets and why others are handled through arrangements that involve lines of authority, internal rules governing transactions, and what we typically refer to as "organizations." Because organizations are ubiquitous in modern life, it may be difficult to understand the origins of this question. For economists, however, whose point of departure in explaining human behavior is the concept of rational individual choice in free markets, the question about why some transactions are subjected to rules and regulations—as if individuals operating purely on their own behalf would not, contrary to the myth of market purity, attain their economic goals—is no trivial matter. Put differently, under what circumstances do people substitute hierarchical governance of relations, as in the modern firm or organization, for purely atomistic, individualized exchanges? Moreover, what are the attributes of different types of organizations that explain their relative success or failure?

Historians and other alert readers may wish to point out, correctly, that the question of economic organization has been with us for centuries. Surely, much of the debate over socialism versus capitalism necessarily involves broader issues than economic efficiency—trust in authority, notions of freedom and liberty, the role of the state. But economic historians have long been interested in comparing marketlike systems favoring individual choice and free exercise of financial capability to hierarchical systems built around concepts of mutually acceptable coercion aimed to further the common good.[23] To the extent that the choice between markets and other systems of economic and social organization is still arguably the core issue in debates over economic policy writ large, a model that helps illuminate the issues has obvious utility for policy and practice.[24]

Coming at this question from the vantage point of economics, Williamson assumed, first, that efficiency is the principal determinant: whether markets or firms (i.e., organizations with internally structured transactions) are preferred is principally a function of their respective efficiencies at converting resources to output. Second, following in the long and respected tradition of neoclassical economic thinking, Williamson began with the assumption that markets are the default mode and then asked under what conditions nonmarket systems would emerge.[25]

Perhaps most germane to my interests here, Williamson's framework hinges to a significant degree on principles of the cognitive revolution. In particular, he wondered how Simon's principle of bounded rationality—the notion of limited human cognitive ability in the face of objectively complex problems—might be linked to choices in the way people design and execute economic transactions. In other words, *could the debate between market and hierarchy be clarified by attention to cognitive issues like bounded rationality and complexity?*

Simon had opened the door to this line of work by theorizing about organizations generally: "It is only because individual human beings are limited in knowledge, foresight, skill, and time that organizations are useful instruments for the achievement of human purpose."[26] Williamson expanded on this observation in the context of transactions costs. Again, here is a concept that is brushed aside in the conventional economic model: competitive markets work on the assumption that people do not have to overcome costly barriers to participate in them. For example, for a rational consumer to make a choice between two competing products, the relevant information is available without cost (indeed, advertising campaigns are all about providing "relevant" information quickly, cleverly, and unforgettably). Granted, the assumption of zero transaction costs is viewed as just another building block toward valid predictions of economic outcomes and not necessarily as a realistic description of the world as we know it. Nevertheless, for Williamson prediction is as much an issue as it is for any of the neoclassicists, but he showed that outcomes depend significantly on the relative costs associated with carrying out economic transactions in different modes, which are determined in part by their attributes vis-à-vis human cognitive constraints: "The costs of writing and executing complex contracts across a market vary with the characteristics of the human decision makers . . . and the objective properties of the market. . . . [And when neurophysiological and linguistic limitations make it] costly or impossible to identify future contingencies and specify, ex ante, appropriate adaptations thereto, long-term contracts may be supplanted by internal organization."[27]

It is the coupling of human bounded rationality with the objective complexity of the decision environment that triggers the question of preferred organizational mode: if bounded rationality were not an issue (i.e., if the assumption, in microeconomics, of human omniscience is dropped), the predictions about optimality of competitive equilibrium and the superiority of markets would gain considerable validity.

Here again, we come upon a wonderful convergence of psychology and computer science, as in the early days of the cognitive revolution.[28] In the strand of work oriented toward organizational choice, computer models have played a significant role. Not surprisingly, Williamson motivates his framework with the example of the game of chess, the complexity of which rules out what Simon might have called the "objectively rational but procedurally irrational" solution strategy: given that, for a chess game of average length, the number of moves that would have to be evaluated explodes to the "unimaginably vast" (10^{120}, or 10 raised to the 120th power), it is ridiculous to model the rational chess player as one who actually tries to produce the complete list and then picks the "best" sequence of moves.[29]

As in the TSP, the advent of high-speed computing has almost—but not entirely—rendered chess a trivial game. From the standpoint of choosing sensible modes of organizing complex economic transactions, however, the complexity of chess coupled with the bounded rationality of human chess players provides a compelling analogy: the idea implicit in the neoclassical theory that consumers have access to the full information needed to make rational decisions and the brainpower to compute the relative advantages of all their choices may have some predictive value but fails miserably on the criterion of face validity. These considerations become even more salient in the context of competitive strategic behavior on the part of individuals involved in economic transactions, in which the simplicity of self-interest seeking belies a more subtle complex of psychological forces that motivate behavior.

As if bounded rationality and complexity were not sufficient reasons to challenge the positivist model, the introduction of other human traits, such as opportunism (self-interest seeking with guile, in Williamson's lexicon) coupled with other environmental conditions (the evolution of markets into small-numbers bargaining situations), establishes a solid foundation for understanding why coordinated collective action supplants atomistic individual competition as a rational and efficient mode of organization.

It is worthwhile to summarize the key predictions that flow from a cognitively inspired approach to economic organization. First, internal organization enables parties engaged in repeated transactions to "deal with uncertainty/complexity in an adaptive, sequential fashion . . . [which] economize[s] greatly on bounded rationality. Rather than specifying the decision tree exhaustively in advance . . . events are permitted to unfold and attention is restricted to only the actual rather than all possible outcomes."[30] Second, with respect to the linguistic side of bounded rationality (i.e., the difficulty of expressing complex contingencies even when they are known or imagined), internal organization affords a venue for the development of efficient codes that are "employed with confidence by the parties. Complex events are summarized in an informal way by using what may be an idiosyncratic language."[31] Finally, internal organization can promote "convergent expectations," raising the probability that decisions will be more mutually compatible than when individuals are forced to make independent decisions in the face of changing external conditions.[32]

How has this theory of economic organization influenced policy and practice? Although the short answer is "slowly," a number of examples support a more optimistic view about the eventual acceptability of these notions in the world of education policy, organization, and reform.

Preventive Maintenance

The first example comes from the world of industry and, in particular, where *preventive maintenance* is a major problem, especially in high-risk settings. As documented in a recent paper prepared for a symposium on rationality in decisionmaking,[33] a problem faced in a fair number of industrial settings is "the failure to give due consideration to preventive maintenance." This organizational lapse can obviously have severe economic and social consequences: production suffers, as do the potential victims of poorly maintained equipment.

What stands out in the analysis of this issue, however, is not the technology of maintenance, which is rather simple, but rather the constraints on managerial efficiency that derive from constraints on human decisionmaking. As the authors of the study note, "It is difficult to establish and maintain preventive maintenance practices in the face of continuing pressure for immediate production and cost-cutting efficiencies. These difficulties are exacerbated by the mental models of employees . . . that conceptualize highly interdependent, dynamic processes as if they can be reduced to separable functions and discrete events."[34] It appears, in other words, that bounded rationality leads to a kind of slicing-and-dicing of complex problems that gives the illusion of improved cognitive grasp; unfortunately, however, the reduction into mentally manageable segments misleads decisionmakers and ultimately causes the preventive system to fail.

The good news reported in this research is that awareness of this confluence of cognitive, behavioral, and organizational phenomena enabled the development of a successful intervention. The strategy adopted by managers, which required a comprehensive effort to change the way maintenance is perceived at all levels of the organization, resulted in the successful change of "mental models through an experiential game that provides a dynamic environment in which employees receive feedback on old and new practices in ways that encourage learning."[35] It seems, indeed, that the cognitive approach illuminated both the source of the problem and a path to its resolution, the latter based on principles of teaching and learning that emphasize pattern recognition, combination of formal and intuitive judgment, and learning by trial and error.

Effort and Incentives

The second example concerns one of the eternally daunting challenges to the way we understand economic exchange. It is one thing to assume casually that individual behavior is motivated by perceived gains and the desire to improve one's economic, social, or health status. But it is no trivial exercise to estimate the effects on behavior of a wide variety of extrinsic and intrinsic rewards that could logically be assumed to matter. In short, what is the relationship between *effort and incentives?*

Conventional wisdom about the nature of work, backed by neoclassical labor economics, has it that stronger incentives—in the form of earnings, primarily—lead to increased effort and that increased effort leads to improved performance. But experimental research that takes behavioral (psychological) assumptions seriously yields some important nuances and caveats to the conventional theory. For example, although it is correct that higher incentives can lead to increased effort, it is by no means certain that these added incentives improve performance. Behavioral economists, whose models derive largely from the convergence of economic and cognitive science, have studied this problem experimentally, and their results are both entertaining and theoretically important.

The authors of one well-known study cleverly exploited an area of human endeavor for which there is abundant observation and exquisitely detailed quantitative data: sports.[36] In their study of basketball free throws, they were able to hypothesize that if extrinsic incentives mattered to players' performance, then it would be possible to estimate the strength of those incentives by comparing how well they do under different game situations. The logic here goes like this: Let's assume that how well basketball players do is at least partly a function of their wish to remain competitive in the sports market and ensure that their hefty contracts are renewed. It follows, then, that when more is at stake for a team and more people are watching, the incentive for improved shooting accuracy will go up. The question, though, is whether that kind of incentive pressure is good or bad for performance. Basketball free throws are a particularly good focus for this kind of study because there is relative calm surrounding the player at the line and the assessment of his (or her) performance is less confounded and more easily measured than when there are multiple arms and bodies intentionally getting in the way. And there is sufficient evidence that how well players do during playoffs makes a significant difference in their postseason marketability, as compared to their overall performance during the regular season.

So the researchers had a lovely combination of plausible assumptions, good evidence to guide their basic hypothesis, and just the right kind of objective data to enable a rigorous statistical design. They found, indeed, that during playoff games, when incentives are higher, *shooting accuracy fell in comparison to the regular season.* This led the authors to conclude that "choking" in sports may be a useful metaphor—with behavioral explanations—for the organization of work and the structuring of incentive systems more generally. Without belaboring the details, the convergence of complex psychological phenomena with standard economic reasoning sheds bright new light on a matter of fundamental importance to the organization of work and the formulation of policies intended to raise productivity and performance.

Human Capital

The final example is drawn from research on an important question facing modern industrial economies: namely, the degree to which profit-making firms can (or should) be expected to invest in the ongoing training of their workforces. Put simply, the question is this: under what circumstances would we expect to observe *firm-sponsored education and training* of employees? Here again, consideration of behavioral and cognitive variables can alter the conventional answer.

In the neoclassical theory of "human capital," a key prediction is that firms will *not* pay for training of their employees in general skills that are, by definition, portable to other firms.[37] The logic is transparent: if workers can be poached away by firms that do not make the training investment, then the firm that does invest will not benefit from the increased productivity that presumably attaches to such training. Because earnings are assumed to be set in the market, the training firm has no choice but to pay a wage similar to the one paid by the nontraining firm. But having laid out the training money, the more generous firm loses out compared to its rivals and, over time, cannot afford to continue the training program. The bottom line is that some kind of coercive policy intervention is needed if the goal is to have firms provide general ongoing formation of the workforce.[38]

The elegance of this theory notwithstanding, empirical evidence about the actual training expenditures in medium and large enterprises suggests that something else may be going on. "When Nell P. Eurich undertook her study of education programs in American business corporations during the early 1980's, she discovered a $60-billion operation that extended from the elementary training programs of lines people of the Bell telephone system to the complex training programs associated with the research activities of IBM, Texas Instruments, and Wang Computing."[39]

Some colleagues and I became interested in this problem and found a promising explanation in terms of Williamson's organizational framework. In our model we hypothesized that, over time, employees and owners become more mutually dependent than is typically assumed by economic theory, and that this dependence limits the competitive forces that would otherwise determine wages and employment. As workers and managers accrue information about each others' skills, performance, and motivations, they are able to use that knowledge to strategic advantage, which gradually leads to a kind of bilateral dependency and a much less "free market" in which workers and firms are sorted and selected. Simply put, the *reality* of decisionmaking and the psychology of human interactions blur the contours of that imaginary marketplace in which buyers and sellers meet and magically find their equilibrium prices.

There is more, however, that relates to the training-investment decision. As workers develop skills that would be portable to other firms, they inevitably increase their stock of human capital relevant to their current firm, which includes those perhaps less tangible qualities of team spirit and personal attachment that strengthen their bond to that firm and reduce the likelihood that they will simply bolt. The key here is that in the process of acquiring skills in training—even skills relevant beyond the gates of their current workplace—workers' ties to the firm in which the training is provided are strengthened: issues of loyalty, the perception that the company is "looking out for them," and notions of "belonging" are inherent in many formal training programs. The bottom line, then, is that both workers and firms benefit when the firm invests in skills development, *even when the skills are quite generalizable and portable to rival firms.*

Using an approach that accounts for cognitive and behavioral variables, we were able to explain observed expenditures on formal training and education (using data from a survey of scientific and technical personnel) and hint at a number of plausible policy implications that would not be obvious from the conventional human-capital model.[40] In a nutshell, policy options vary considerably depending on which assumptions govern predictions about private-sector propensities to invest in a public good such as education and training, and conscious attention to cognitively inspired assumptions can make a substantial difference.

I have included here only three examples of ways in which attention to cognitive attributes of decisionmakers who face objectively complex problems enables both more plausible assumptions and more reliable predictions than are typical under the behaviorist principles of neoclassical economics and organization theory.[41] The literature is already large, and the imprint on policy thinking has been significant, if not quite determinative.[42] The central lesson is this: most of the policy issues to which the cognitively inspired revision of economic and organization theory has been applied are no more complex than the world of schools and schooling. The confluence of environmental complexities in education—political and historical preference for decentralized governance; rapidly changing demographic and economic conditions of the population served by the school system; widely divergent opinions about the purposes of schooling and the definition of achievement; absence of agreed-upon metrics by which to judge performance of students, teachers, schools, school systems, states, and the nation; and evolving conceptions of the appropriate content of curricula and their implications for pedagogy—would augur well for an education-policy theory grounded in something other than "objective" rationality. Still, to date scant attention has been paid to the cognitive bounds of educators and education policymakers and the effects of appreciating these bounds on the design, execution, and evaluation of education reform. Filling this gap is my goal in the chapters that follow.

CHAPTER 2

◻

Complexity by Design

It is the provisions for public education which, from the very first, throw into clearest relief the originality of American civilization.

> *Alexis de Tocqueville,* Democracy in America, *1835*

When one tells a foreign visitor that we have tens of thousands of local school boards with vast powers over the elementary schools and the high schools, he is apt to say, "this is not a system but a chaos." To which I always reply: "But it works, most of us like it, and it appears to be as permanent a feature of our society as most of our political institutions."

> *James Bryant Conant, as quoted by Daniel Boorstin,*
> The Americans: The Democratic Experience, *1973*

At a meeting in Washington, D.C., in 1999, hosted by the president of the National Academy of Sciences, the French minister of education, Claude Allègre, himself a distinguished scientist and a member of the Academy, outlined the French approach to education reform: "In the spring I decided to adopt the 'hands-on' method for teaching science. By the beginning of the new school year, all French students were learning from the new curriculum." The minister's awestruck audience, a small group of American education-policy experts and scientists frustrated by the persistently poor showing of American students on comparative tests of mathematics and science, could hardly contain their envy. One of them mumbled audibly, "If only we had central authority in our education system, if only we had that kind of control." Others nodded and exchanged sad glances of resignation. Allègre sympathized with his confrères who yearned for national goals and standards, but he offered a diplomat's wise caution. "Yes, it's true," he said, "we have substantial power vested in central government. And that allows us to change teaching and learning relatively quickly and efficiently. But don't forget: when the government has that kind of concentrated power, so does the opposition." Allègre knew what he was saying. Six months later he was ousted under pressure brought by the powerful and centrally organized teachers' union.[1]

VIVE LA DIFFÉRENCE

It is a truism that a society's education system is a reflection of its culture, history, and politics. That French education is controlled by a centralized governmental bureaucracy is therefore not surprising. The French prefer significantly more government involvement and regulatory control of their economy and society than would be imaginable in the United States. What should be surprising—at least to students of economic history who have pondered the American aversion to bureaucracy, distrust of central authority, and religious-like zeal for free enterprise—is the survival of public bureaucracy in the provision of education in the United States. True, American capitalism has evolved a peculiarly ingenious system of regulated free enterprise (oxymoron intended), which some economic historians credit with the survival of the system;[2] and it is also the case that purely free and competitive markets are as rare in the real world—even in the United States—as a perfect vacuum is in the physics laboratory. Nevertheless, it is fair to say that market competition is the ideal in the American vision of economic organization, and that the burden of proof usually rests with those who advocate for a bureaucratic "visible hand" to guide and constrain economic and social transactions.[3] Hence the surprise about American education, a frigate of public bureaucracy afloat in a sea of free enterprise.

The contrast with France needs work, however. There are at least three issues at play: whether a school system is public or private, whether decisions are made centrally or locally, and whether the system is governed (and held accountable) bureaucratically or by principles of market competition. In theory, there is no particular reason why these features must come in specific combinations, although typically bureaucracy is understood as the public sector and government is understood to be the national sovereign.

On the first dimension, public versus private, the U.S. school system is not very different from most others in the world, including the French. In the economist's shorthand, education is an essential ingredient of human capital, which most societies recognize as an appropriate target for public investment supported by some kind of coercive taxation. Given the American faith in its private sector for so many other goods and services—including some, arguably, with attributes of "public goods"—it is noteworthy that education is still considered by the overwhelming majority of Americans to be a legitimate (if messy) public enterprise.[4]

With respect to degree of centralization, the comparison needs still more unpacking. It is certainly true that France has a national education system with roots deep in the country's history and culture, in stark contrast to the United States, where the experiment with national educational goals and standards is a recent (and controversial) phenomenon and the idea of federal control of schooling is considered both a constitutional and a cultural taboo. But this is the wrong comparative frame; it would make more sense to consider the states individually or in groups rather than the massively complex union of 50 states with a combined population roughly five times that of France. Accounting for differences in population and geographic size as well as historical traditions that have shaped the political identities of the states, it would be more productive to contrast the education system of France with those in, say, New York or New England. (Indeed, international comparisons of achievement take on a very different light when U.S. assessment scores are disaggregated by state.) Viewed through this lens, the comparison again suggests more similarity than difference, given that each state has responsibilities for curriculum, finance, and governance not unlike those vested in the central ministry in Paris. Granted, the specifics of school management vary both within the United States and between the various states and foreign nations. Our system of locally elected school boards (there are now about 15,000), with enormous power for setting policy, hiring teachers and administrators, and monitoring student learning, is unique in the world. But a striking feature of the U.S. system is how it reflects a best-of-both-worlds solution to the question of centralized versus localized control. In the tradition of conflict and conciliation between the ethos of one nation and the governmental power of the states, the U.S. school system has evolved into a decentralized system of state-run bureaucracies. (System may be the wrong word here; hodgepodge is more apt. I shall return later to the tension between federal and state control.)

On the third dimension, market versus bureaucracy, the comparison between the United States and France (along with most industrialized democracies) is again interesting more for the similarities than the differences. Notwithstanding the fervor of arguments for privatization and competition in U.S. schooling, which should have obvious receptor sites in a society so dominated by the ethos of free enterprise, bureaucracy has demonstrated remarkable stamina. The proportion of students who attend private schools (both religious and secular) has hovered around 12 percent of the total since data on the issue began to be collected.[5] Despite all the attention given to voucher, charter, and choice initiatives in the past 20 years—with increasingly shrill polemics touting their organizational and educational advantages—rigorous empirical evidence of their effectiveness is, at best, sketchy.[6] Again, what is remarkable is that despite all our historical and cultural appreciation for private enterprise, our school systems haven't budged much in that direction.

Toward Procedural Rationality

It is not my goal here to settle the argument over choice and vouchers in the U.S. reform agenda. Nevertheless, I offer two observations pertinent to the theme of this book. First, current experiments with public school choice, as well as the prominent role that choice plays in the landmark No Child Left Behind Act of 2001, again reflect a certain pragmatic streak in American politics that favors middle-ground solutions over ideological rigidities. Just as the country has evolved a system of decentralized bureaucracies, it seems in this case to be experimenting with a best-of-both-worlds solution that blends public accountability with the virtues of market competition. Charter schools are, after all, nonprofit organizations subject to at least some form of modified public control. The simple point, again, is that Americans behave as if they favor compromise over the extremes, even if the rhetoric to which they are exposed is usually less moderate.[7]

Second, I shall go one perhaps hazardous step farther and argue that the survival and growth of our public, bureaucratic system of school governance suggests neither a failure of representative democracy nor political inertia but rather the collective will of American families, voters, and their legislative representatives. Americans have always been free to change their system of educational governance, which is a good thing, given the gross injustices that have been corrected only by the sweat of grassroots activists, lawyers, and politicians committed to social change. The fact that we have maintained the public bureaucratic model suggests, other things being equal, a preference over alternative modes in which education could be organized and provided.[8] In view of the chronic pathologies affecting the system—inequality in resource allocation and gaps in student achievement being the most pernicious—the perceived value of schooling as provided in our fragmented and somewhat chaotic public system must indeed be formidable. Without compelling evidence of political failure on a grand scale, it follows axiomatically that the survival of the public education system must be based at least partially on a broad social calculation that the benefits exceed the costs. And if it is true that Americans are free to choose how to organize their schools, that they are free to define the goals and purposes of education as they see fit, and that they have sufficient information to guide their choices, then on the whole it might be argued that the system is collectively rational.[9]

But only procedurally so. For even if the existing organization of schooling can be called rational, based on the assumed benefit-cost calculus, it is at best a definition of rationality based on satisficing rather than optimizing decisions. This is Simon's idea, that is, that human beings, faced with complex problems and limited mental capacity, choose reasonably good strategies rather than perfect ones, the latter requiring unreasonable time and/or inordinately elaborate solutions. The combination of complexity and uncertainty that characterizes most decisions at all levels of the education system—decisions that must be made by mortals with bounds on their cognitive capacities—makes the traveling-salesman problem appear trivial by comparison.[10] Which allows me to end this series of digressions into comparative education and return to the irony motivating this book: through cognitive science we have come to understand and appreciate the extent to which practices of teaching and learning require a blend of formal, experiential, and intuitive knowledge, but we have not yet formally extended those lessons to modeling (and improving) the practice of education policy and governance.

This chapter takes a step in that direction, proposing procedural rationality, a concept that has spawned important changes in conventional theories of economic and social governance, as a frame in which to understand and set education policy.[11] At the risk of repetition, the specific argument is this: given the myriad and ill-defined objectives of education, a complex political environment designed to prevent the concentration of central governmental authority, changing theories of teaching and learning born of increasingly sophisticated cognitive and behavioral science, inherent limits to even the most advanced and innovative tools of measurement and evaluation, bounds on the capacities of educators and education leaders to understand and solve the problems they face, and opportunistic inclinations of even the most virtuous actors in the education system, it is no wonder that reform initiatives steeped in the rhetoric of rapid and comprehensive change always seem to fall short of the lofty goals with which they are pronounced.

My proposal, then, is to adjust the theory of action underlying education reform and research, from one with implicit tones of optimization and objective rationality toward one that assumes conditions of complexity coupled with cognitive limits of educational decisionmakers; from one that inevitably disappoints researchers and reformers to one that embraces without shame or embarrassment the ideal of reasonable strategies based on appropriate deliberation; from one that sees inevitable failure in every imperfect proposal to one that tolerates incremental improvement, steady albeit slow progress, and continual evaluation. Embedded here is a language issue: the rhetorical flourish that attends most reform proposals is, itself, evidence of a system beset with social-psychological complexity; a theory built around the concept of satisficing includes moderation of language in which goals are articulated, policies enacted, and public expectations shaped.[12]

To make my case I will review here three long-standing issues—test-based accountability, national assessment, and the science of education research. I will suggest that most policies (and proposed policies) in these arenas have always reflected uneasy compromises over multiple and complex goals; that objectively optimal solutions to the most interesting education-policy questions are a dangerous chimera; and that therefore the pursuit of reasonable compromise strategies should be the acceptable norm.[13] Such a shift in the way one thinks about, designs, and evaluates education policy requires a new pact between policymakers and their publics, which will be the focus of chapter 3.

TESTING POLICY AS SATISFICING

I begin again with a true story that will perhaps sound all too familiar. The results of a test administered to thousands of American students were dismaying: out of 57,873 possible answers, students answered only 17,216 correctly and accumulated 35,947 errors in punctuation in the process. One child said that rivers in North Carolina and Tennessee run in opposite directions because of the "will of God." Now, if you are feeling that recurring miasma that comes from reading about the sorry condition of schooling in the United States, you can take comfort, perhaps, from knowing that these results are not current. I am not quoting the latest results of NAEP or PISA or TIMSS, but rather from a report about one of the first written examinations ever given in American schools—circa 1845.[14]

For a system often accused of faddishness, the longevity of America's romance with testing is extraordinary. I argued earlier that the organization of schooling generally reflects society's political choices, culture, and history. No less so with testing, a linchpin of the system that reflects a number of powerful but frequently incompatible cultural and historical norms: faith in science and technology (in this case the science of psychological and educational measurement) to provide practical answers to complex problems, preference for meritocracy over aristocracy as the principal mechanism through which economic opportunity is distributed, insistence on reliable evidence for the effectiveness of programs funded from public coffers, protection of state and local values from overreaching federal involvement in curriculum and pedagogy, and belief in tangible incentives to motivate maximal performance of teachers and students.

Thus, while popular histories typically demonize the testing industry and blame persistent inequality—in resources, opportunities, and academic performance—at least in part on the allegedly unfair content and format of tests,[15] the story is more complex. Using uniform written examinations to gauge student learning and school system performance was not a plot devised by authoritarians bent on squelching liberal education and excluding the masses. Rather, it was a brilliant innovation of common-school reformers—Horace Mann, Samuel Gridley Howe, and their allies—who were committed to an unprecedented expansion of the education franchise and to fairness and efficiency in its execution. They favored written testing over oral examinations largely on grounds of fairness, reaching that position long before the invention of reliability statistics and the advent of modern psychometrics; they discovered the potent force of test results in exposing incompetencies of teachers and headmasters long before "test-based accountability" became fashionable; and they celebrated the efficiency of written tests to guide student classification and manage ever-growing school populations long before the invention of multiple-choice items and machine-scorable answer sheets.[16]

They were also the first to miscalculate the unintended effects of reliance on test scores as tools of reform and were therefore (and, I am willing to assume, unwittingly) the progenitors of a trend in test misuse that many would argue has always been a stain on the otherwise sound use of measurement methodology.[17]

The Tug of Scores

Since those early days of written examinations in New England, testing technology has evolved considerably, and arguments for and against test use have drifted back and forth across political boundaries. But the underlying concept of measurement as a driver of education reform has remained remarkably stable, notwithstanding deep-seated ambivalences that have fueled a seemingly endless debate. My goal here is not to refute the often exaggerated claims, positive and negative, about the uses and effects of tests in American society. Rather, I want to argue that a procedurally rational testing policy would (like tests themselves) assume inherent imperfections and inevitable errors and would strive to define reasonable—albeit at times disappointing—policy outcomes.

The tensions and complexities surrounding test design and use establish a good case for something other than optimization as the metaphor for how testing policy decisions are made. It may be best to imagine the paragraphs that follow as describing orbiting satellites that occasionally collide, on shaky trajectories, with somewhat hapless but well-meaning policymakers responding to mutually incompatible demands of their constituents and trying against tough odds to set the dials on their controls to the steady state. Viewed from another planet, our world of testing is indeed one of constant inspiration—and perspiration.

We begin with an accepted tenet of the assessment and measurement profession. Standardized testing can be an important policy tool in the ongoing American experiment to provide quality education to an increasingly diverse and growing population. But the economic advantages of large-scale and machine-scored tests are not (yet) possible with assessments that capture cognitive functioning and student achievement in greater depth. Hence, if a purpose of testing is to provide reliable data about individual student performance system wide, economic considerations will tend to favor tests that emphasize basic skills rather than complex thought.[18]

Tests are much more than measurement tools. They are seen, increasingly, as tools for changing human behavior. Indeed, embedded in the notion of test-based accountability is a theory of action that resonates (perhaps too easily) with anyone who has ever studied for an important exam: tests create incentives for changed behavior, one hopes in the direction of harder work by teachers and students. But there is substantial empirical evidence that if test scores are associated with extrinsic rewards and sanctions, teachers and students will substitute test-taking techniques for the underlying skills and knowledge the tests are designed to estimate, which can easily lead to "score inflation" that compromises the validity of inferences drawn from the results. In more extreme situations, there is evidence (theoretical and empirical) of incentives for behavior ranging from coaching, which may have at least some salutary effects, to outright cheating. There is currently no equivalent of a well-calibrated thermostat that would allow the incentives to "heat up" just enough to produce desirable outcomes in classrooms without unintended negative side effects; worse yet, although side effects are known to exist, there is no tool to estimate which students and which schools are the most vulnerable potential victims.[19]

The seemingly insatiable demand for testing by politicians and the public stems from legitimate principles of democratic accountability and fairness in resource allocation, the basic idea being to ascertain whether all students have access to equally good teaching (and other resources) using measures that provide a fair basis for comparison. Using results of assessments to monitor performance of schools or school systems and to hold teachers and principals accountable, without controlling for such exogenous sources of variation in student learning as family background and socioeconomic status, is both unscientific and unfair. But the inclusion of control variables to account for sources of variation beyond the control of teachers and schools may be misconstrued as tolerance for inequality, the (perhaps unintended) establishment of differential expectations for affluent and poor students, and misplaced emphasis on the role of genes or other relatively immutable traits in explaining achievement differences.[20]

The natural tendency (especially in a society concerned with economic efficiency) to favor dual or multiuse technologies has led to almost uncontrollable urges to use tests for multiple purposes simultaneously. While it is true that supplying teachers and students with information relevant to classroom teaching and learning, monitoring system-wide educational performance, and informing selection, placement, and credentialing decisions share a common theme of information, the types of information elicited by different tests and the types of decisions they are intended to support are fundamentally different. If tests designed to assess certain aspects of student learning are applied toward purposes for which they are not necessarily well suited, the result can be a distortion in the validity of scores and confusion on the part of decisionmakers. Hence, one of the most vexing challenges has been to align various measurement technologies to specific purposes for which they are designed and validated and to prevent or minimize misuse.[21]

Standardized tests can provide useful information if they are designed and administered in accordance with established scientific standards, and the technical quality of tests has improved significantly thanks to the science of psychometrics. Ironically, however, as the science of testing has become more sophisticated in response to demands for validity, reliability, and fairness, popular misconceptions about the precision of test scores have grown worse. In a word, quantitative data often appear "scientific" and are therefore presumed to be more precise than they really are. Because scores will always be vulnerable to various sources of error (regardless of how good the tests are), important decisions should never rely solely on a single test. This is indeed a staple of the professional measurement community's code of professional conduct.[22]

In view of these tensions, it is hardly surprising that the history of testing in the United States is fraught with dissent, distrust, dispute, and disappointment. Unfortunately, there is a tendency to emphasize these four D's at the expense of a set of three R's—rigor, reason, and rationality—that could characterize test use. Frequently, the debate over testing is vulgarized by reference to the "anti-testers" and the "pro-testers," whereas in more nuanced discussions it is cast in terms of a grand social-welfare balancing act. In other words, even if test-based accountability helps some unknown number of students in low-performing schools, this comes at the expense of causing some unmeasured degree of harm to the system as a whole—as if the inevitability of social costs is sufficient to guide policy without consideration for the possibility of compensating social benefits.[23]

My recommendation for a procedurally rational reformulation of the problem hinges on two sets of assumptions. First, it is crucial that policymakers and the general public understand the interplay between certain (perhaps immutable) qualities of the political and social environment of testing, technical constraints on the precision of measurement, and the opportunistic inclinations of test takers and decisionmakers. Without such understanding, we will be sentenced to perpetual dispute and disappointment regarding the uses and meaning of test results.

Second, it is crucial to reframe the testing policy debate with emphasis on a few fundamental principles: whether distortions that arise from the coupling of environmental, technical, and human factors are predictable; whether the magnitude and distribution of the effects of the distortion can be estimated ex ante; whether the predictable distortions can be corrected using statistical or other means; and whether, in the end, the distortions necessarily outweigh whatever benefits are expected or predicted from the testing program in question.

The Politics of Testing and the Testing of Politics

In a recent paper for a conference sponsored by the Educational Testing Service, I wrote that "however appealing intuitively and philosophically is the idea that we can have a national ethos of education while preserving and nurturing state and local instincts, finding the balance has always required a good bit of operational compromise and linguistic deftness."[24] I was writing about one of the more recent and extraordinary juggling efforts, which advanced the curious proposition that psychometrics could solve a fundamental problem of American federalism. The story is worth revisiting, especially as it illustrates, again, the significance of compromise strategies when multiple goals are incompatible, and the need to pursue solutions that may be short of perfect but possibly better than any of the known alternatives. In retrospect, a strident debate over what seemed to be an arcane statistical question would have been more constructive had it been imbued with basic principles of procedural rationality. The revelation that a certain strategy is flawed is not enough. The key question must be, "How bad *are* the flaws?"

In January 1997 President Clinton announced his intention to develop and administer voluntary national tests of reading and mathematics in three grades. With hindsight, one can now draw an almost straight line from the test-based reforms of the 1970s (minimum-competency testing), through the post–*A Nation at Risk* standards initiatives of the 1980s and the development of national educational goals, to the Clinton proposal for federally sponsored tests intended to provide nationally relevant measures of academic performance. It was not the first time that national leaders looked at the myriad forms of testing going on in the states while remaining unable to figure out much about the condition of schooling, nor was it the first time that testing was made the centerpiece of reform.[25]

At the time, however, the initiative was as radical a proposition as any in the history of school-reform policy, principally because it called on the federal government to lead the test-design program. Not surprisingly, therefore, opposition to the idea mounted swiftly and stereophonically: from the left came complaints of potential adverse impact and discrimination, and from the right came complaints about federal encroachment on states' rights. As one of the wittier education-policy wonks of the era quipped, "There are only two things wrong with the voluntary national test: half the country hates the word test and the other half hates the word national."[26]

It is important to underscore the context for this initiative and why it caused such a furor in Congress, in the states, in teacher associations, in parent groups, and in the research community. If there is a one-line warning to policymakers to be gleaned from the complex history of American education policy, it might be this: the concept of national is tolerable, but those who confound national with federal do so at their peril. For example, it was not until 1994 that Congress codified in federal law (Goals 2000) a set of eight "national educational goals," six of which were taken from the Charlottesville summit of 1989, a landmark political event that brought together the National Governors' Association (chaired by Governor Bill Clinton) and the White House (under President George H. W. Bush) with business and industry leaders, union heads, and other education statespersons. But even the national goals did not simplify or clarify the question of authority. It was still up to the states and districts to shape the goals according to their own specific ideals, to develop their own challenging content and performance standards, and to implement the spirit of the newly articulated national educational ethos according to locally determined preferences. The question of whether and how the tremendous variety in state definitions of "challenging" would be aggregated into a measure of national progress was not directly tackled.

And there were no obvious exemplars from which to borrow ideas for a blueprint. It was already quite clear, however, that given the peculiar genius of the decentralized bureaucratic system, national standards would have to derive up from the aggregation of state and local definitions of what is valued in education, and never down from those lofty and mistrusted heights of federal authority. A perhaps less obvious corollary, however, is that any such aggregation will always be imperfect.[27]

Imperfection, however, was sufficient for many education researchers (myself among them) to dismiss, albeit regretfully, at least one of the strategies proposed as a compromise between the quest for national measures and the preservation of state and local decisionmaking. The proposal came in the form of a rebuttal to President Clinton's voluntary national test initiative, articulated most forcefully by William Goodling, an otherwise moderate and mild-mannered congressman from Pennsylvania. A former schoolteacher, Goodling had risen to the powerful position of chair of the House Education and Workforce Committee, devoting much of his career to the improvement of education. He had no problem with test-based accountability as a prod for reform, but he was driven to uncharacteristic anger—seething, in fact—at the prospect of a federally run testing program, which, in his view, was tantamount to the imposition of a federal curriculum.[28]

Goodling asked an intuitively appealing question, one that embodied a fundamental tension in the American system: Would it not be possible to allow states and districts to continue using their own tests (the decentralization impulse) but to score them on the same scale (the national impulse)? Through the magic of psychometrics, myriad configurations of content reflected in curricula of the 50 states and summarized in items on almost as many tests would be distilled into a reporting system that allowed Americans wherever they live to see how their children are doing and to make valid comparative judgments about the performance of their schools. It sounded simple and logical, and, as it turned out, it really wasn't rocket science—it was harder.

The arranged marriage of measurement technology and political expedience did not exactly bring the parties happily to the altar. Rather, it sparked a violent dispute (in rhetoric only, mercifully) between those favoring the one-test solution and those insisting on continued commercial and political variety. It also led to inclusion in the law of a requirement for a National Research Council (NRC) study to explore whether "an equivalency scale can be developed that would allow test scores from commercially available standardized tests and State assessments to be compared with each other and the National Assessment of Educational Progress."[29] For a brief time, then, the adversaries ceased fire while the scientific merits of the proposition could be evaluated by a neutral and respected scientific organization.

The NRC convened a committee of distinguished educators and statisticians with expertise in test design, validity analysis, and "equivalency" or "linking" (the mathematics of cross-test comparisons of scores and their interpretation). The group was fortunate to have as chair Paul Holland, a world-class mathematical statistician committed to producing an impartial, clearly written, and usable report. They approached their charge with a deep appreciation for the historical and political context of the technical question that Congress had posed:

> Viewed through [the] lens of our unique experiment in pluralism and federalism, the question motivating this study is both predictable and sensible. Given the rich and increasingly diverse array of tests used by states and districts in pursuit of improved educational performance, can information be provided on a common scale? Can scores on one test be made interpretable in terms of scores on other tests? Can we have more uniform data about student performance from our healthy

hodgepodge of state and local programs? Can linkage be the testing equivalent of "e pluribus unum?"[30]

After deliberations that lasted only about nine months, involving intensive review of the technical literature and consideration of every possible methodological nuance, the committee's answer was a blunt "no." Developing a new scale to link all the existing tests would not be feasible and would not make sense; using the existing NAEP scale and achievement levels would not work either. (A faint glimmer of hope had emerged from a much-reduced formulation of the problem: under limited conditions, links between some or clusters of tests might be defensible for a limited set of inferences.)

The findings rested on evidence of constraints inherent in the existing ecology of testing in the United States, which should by now sound familiar. Because tests inevitably cover only portions of a domain of interest, such as mathematics, test developers must make choices in what to cover and with what emphasis. "When content differences are significant, scores from one test provide poor estimates of scores on another test [and] any calculated linkage between them would have little practical meaning and would be misleading for many uses."[31] As state and local authority for education is strengthened, so too is the likelihood of increased variation and innovation in test design. The effects of differences in test format on the validity of inferences from linked scores are difficult to predict.

The plot thickens. Because all test results are estimates of performance subject to some level of error, the question of whether score reliability is compromised by linking has important practical consequences. "If test A, with a large margin of error, is linked with test B, which is much more precise, the score of a person who took test A still has the margin of error of test A even when [the result] is reported in terms of the scale of test B."[32]

Next, there is another encroachment of reality, the role of human judgment and decisionmaking in shaping the validity and utility of testing technology. Evidence abounds on the threats to test validity caused by differences in the uses to which test results are applied. Given the variability in the purposes of testing and the application of results to policy decisions in the states and districts, there is danger that simple test linking will be misleading and unstable over time.

The pessimism in the NRC report was surprising, given the natural penchant of scientists to be hopeful for technical solutions to complex problems.[33] Under Holland's firm guidance, the committee sought valiantly to find some way to give even a faintly positive answer to the question it had been posed. "We reached these conclusions despite our appreciation of the potential value of a technical solution to the dual challenges of maintaining diversity and innovation in testing while satisfying growing demands for nationally benchmarked data on individual student performance."[34]

There was an eleventh-hour reprieve, however, inspired by committee member Frederick Mosteller, recognized widely as perhaps the preeminent social statistician of his generation. In his own modest way, Mosteller caused a small intellectual earthquake by noting that potential flaws or compromises to validity and reliability might not be sufficient to dismiss the linkage solution. The question for Fred was more subtle: By how much would score meanings be compromised under various linkage schemes? In other words, Mosteller was willing to concede that linkage was not costless, but he cautioned the committee against ignoring any potential benefits too blithely. It was beyond the scope and resources of the original committee to collect and analyze the data needed to answer Mosteller's question, although he did open the door to a slight reinterpretation of the original charge and to the possibility that under some circumstances linkage of some tests might be feasible.[35]

For me, Mosteller's query was about more than the validity of linked tests. With a bit of rephrasing, it was (and is) an entrée into thinking about procedural rationality in testing policy. Given the formidable obstacles that prevent development of a scale to integrate multiple measures of educational performance—that is, to provide an optimal solution to the equivalency problem—what are the methods that will produce an acceptably low level of distortion in validity and reliability? What would constitute satisfactory levels of equivalency for specific intended uses of the results? What risks from potential misunderstanding of the linked scores might be tolerable in view of anticipated benefits? These questions can be extended to consideration of other education policies besides those related to testing and equivalence; again, they reflect the importance of tolerating reasonable rather than optimal solutions.

As I will argue in the next chapter, accepting this policy-analysis framework requires, among other things, a pact between producers and users of scientific knowledge. The central challenge faced by researchers is the delineation of boundaries to the validity of imperfect (satisficing) solutions, explication of constraints imposed by the political or cultural context, and rigorous analyses of the plausibility, utility, benefits, and costs of alternative solutions, even to the most apparently intractable questions. The central challenge facing policymakers, in turn, is to appreciate that science is, by its nature, an exercise in skepticism and that researchers' penchant for inquiry and the empirical refutation of plausible hypotheses should not be mistaken for an apology for the status quo. Which brings me to the question of scientific research in education, my third example of an education-policy debate that would be well served by considerations of procedural rationality.

THE SCIENCE OF THE SCIENCE OF EDUCATION

It might be apparent from the preceding discussion that my argument for procedural rationality simultaneously involves description and prescription: I use the concept to suggest how decisions are made, and also how they should be made. It follows that my attempt to lay the groundwork for a theory of educational organization and governance is essentially a proposition about the science of education; it is based on assumptions about human information processing and complexity that emerge from cognitive science. If successful, the theory will find a place alongside the "new institutional economics" and the contemporary theory of organizations.

But what does "successful" mean? How can one know if the propositions advanced here are reasonable, logical, and predictive? Whether it is Shulman's "wisdom of practice" or my expropriation of "procedural rationality," are the theories testable? If so, how? At the risk of some circularity in reasoning, let me suggest that procedural rationality is not just a theoretical construct relevant to human decisionmaking and organization, as I have been arguing. It is also a way to characterize scientific inquiry generally and the development of rules of evidence specifically. My point here is, essentially, to practice what I preach. In order to evaluate the strengths and weaknesses of my suggested framework, we could actually apply its core principles. In other words, we can be procedurally rational in the evaluation of procedural rationality. The notion that seeking reasonably good answers to complex questions is as good or better than holding out for an idealized optimum is quite amenable to devising a strategy and methodology for validating the theory of procedural rationality in educational organization and governance. Given the inherent complexity surrounding educational decisions and the known imperfections in measurement methodology, what are the appropriate—as opposed to ideal—standards of evidence necessary to evaluate the validity of this (or any) theory of education?[36]

Indeed, procedural rationality then becomes an even more robust apparatus: it helps model the real complexities of education policymaking, suggests a realistic approach to evaluating the qualities of such a model, and opens the door to a more eclectic approach to policy analysis and education-program evaluation generally. The question about evidentiary standards and methodology in education research connects to familiar concepts of cognitive science: In view of the evidence about human decisionmaking under assumptions of complexity and bounded rationality (the traveling-salesman problem is perhaps still the best metaphor), how do considerations of time, cost, and utility of the resulting information lead toward a procedurally rational calculus for selecting appropriate methods of scientific inquiry?

Politics of Science

Methodology, sampling, causation and correlation, and evidentiary standards have become flashpoints in the education-policy and reform zeitgeist. Both the process through which the education-research debate has evolved and the formulation of emerging principles to guide decisions about the scientific nature of education research can benefit from the framework being proposed in these chapters. I shall consider first the process and its policy context.

Does the repeated—some might say obsessive—appearance of the phrase "scientifically based research" in the No Child Left Behind Act suggest yet another attempt at grand compromise over compelling but mutually incompatible goals? Whether education is or should be a science has been debated for over 100 years. The most recent round began innocently enough, with the framers of major federal legislation codifying in law their appetite for empirical evidence as the basis for educational policy and programs. But the effect has been to re-open old wounds and launch a new round of battles over the science of education. The impetus for more and better scientific research was fueled in part by acknowledgment from the education-research community that the field is crowded with low-quality work,[37] but the principal driving force has been the frustration felt by policymakers with the cacophony of reform initiatives that are frequently perceived to be unencumbered by any evidence of effects.

There is a more positive or charitable explanation, too. Accumulated research evidence on the teaching of reading, summarized in a major National Research Council report and subsequently reinforced in a congressionally mandated panel review,[38] prompted leading members of Congress to call for more research to inform education-reform policies. Simply put, the awareness that research had produced useful answers led federal policymakers to want more.[39] The impending reauthorization of the Federal Office of Education Research and Improvement (OERI) was a perfect opportunity to codify the government's commitment to rigorous scientific evidence and to signal a laudable goal that could be embraced in Congress by both sides of the aisle—namely, to displace at least some of the ideological rhetoric surrounding school reform with factual information derived from careful research.[40] It began with a more narrowly focused effort to "ensure that federal funds for reading education be used in ways that reflected the best available scientific evidence,"[41] which became the guiding principle for the Reading Excellence Act of 1999. But the idea spread, and soon the phrase "scientifically based research" was a linchpin of OERI reauthorization language as well as the landmark No Child Left Behind Act.

While draft language was circulating, penned largely in the offices of Representative Mike Castle (a Republican from Delaware), education researchers as well as social (and even physical) scientists began to worry. Was it proper for politicians to be legislating principles of good science? Were their efforts well intentioned and on the right track? Not surprisingly, the instinctive answer to both questions was as bluntly negative as the NRC's answer had been to Congressman Goodling's question about test linkage. Among so-called qualitative researchers, there was anxiety over funding for ethnographic, historical, and humanistic studies. Even among more quantitatively oriented social scientists, whose repertoires are more likely to include experimental designs of the sort favored by the framers of the OERI reauthorization bill, there was consternation about the intrusion of government in the workings of science.[42]

Scientists on Science

Nevertheless, the education community faced an unfamiliar dilemma. After decades of disappointment in the low level of attention afforded research by congressional appropriators, researchers suddenly had some champions—Representative Castle, research managers at the National Institute of Child Health and Human Development, even President George W. Bush—who insisted that good research had a vital place in the future of America's schools. "To rejoice or to recoil": I wrote with colleagues in a special issue of *Educational Researcher,* "that [was] the question faced by educational researchers. . . . Unprecedented federal legislation exalts scientific evidence . . . but . . . it also inches dangerously toward a prescription of methods and a rigid definition of research quality."[43] Having a spotlight shine on them after years of feeling neglected by government audiences gave education researchers pause. Could they capitalize on the political groundswell that had begun to roll forward and help steer the ship of legislation into safer waters?

In an ideal world, perhaps, scientists might fantasize that norms of inquiry and decisions about methodology are left exclusively to researchers in their laboratories. But in the real world of user-oriented research,[44] scientists whose work is aimed at the improvement of policy and practice have come to understand the significance of negotiated compromises—satisficing solutions—with their public benefactors. The idea that scientists should play a constructive role in shaping the legislation that would ultimately affect their research programs was not novel, nor was the suggestion to ask the National Research Council, which has had a long and distinguished record of contributions to science policy and the federal role in research and development, to weigh in on the debate. But the request to examine the philosophical and practical underpinnings of "scientifically based education research" was special for several reasons.

First, it underscored a shift in the attitude toward education research on the part of the federal government. This was not only a question about how to organize the federal role in education research, which had been addressed in earlier NRC reports; rather, it could be seen as an implicit endorsement of the principle that education research—however it is organized—is a bona fide matter of science. After all, why else involve the National Research Council, the operating arm of the National Academy of Sciences? Second, it put before the NRC a question about the fundamental nature of science—its definition, criteria for judging quality, norms of inquiry, and standards of evidence. In other words, a committee of scientists was asked to engage in what psychologists might call a "metacognitive" task—thinking intensively about their work and their thought. Third, it required scientists who do not usually think about education research, and education researchers who are not accustomed to thinking about the nature of science, to work together toward a consensus position on key principles—and, moreover, to articulate that consensus in order to inform legislation in the making.[45]

I began this discussion by asking whether the evolution of policy regarding education research illustrates the spirit of pragmatic compromise that one sees throughout American education history. At the risk of overstating the case, it is fair to say that, as a result of the NRC report, the final version of the OERI reauthorization was different in important ways from its initial drafts. Moreover, key points of controversy, such as the distinction between qualitative and quantitative inquiry, were at least temporarily settled by language that was jointly influenced by scientists and politicians.[46]

Although it was the OERI policy board (and in particular its very astute chair, Stanford linguist and education researcher Kenji Hakuta) that requested the NRC study, the resulting report covered substantive issues that went well beyond the boundaries of education. Indeed, a distinguished multidisciplinary group chaired by a prominent and wide-ranging social scientist, Richard Shavelson, the committee noted that its initial attempts to single out education for special treatment—on grounds that scientific principles for the physical world cannot be applied to something as complex as schools and students—failed in the face of the evidence. "Ultimately, we failed to convince ourselves that at a fundamental level beyond the differences in specialized techniques and objects of inquiry across the individual sciences, a meaningful distinction could be made among social, physical, and life science research and scientific research in education."[47] This underlying finding does not, of course, mean that the ways in which scientific principles are carried out are identical across all domains of study: "The ways those principles are instantiated—in astrophysics, biochemistry, labor economics, cultural anthropology, or mathematics teaching—depend on the specific features of what is being studied."[48] But the importance of that conclusion cannot be overestimated. It meant that the committee, with the endorsement of the National Research Council, had taken a stand in the old debate over whether education should be accorded the status of a bona fide scientific field.

Rhetoric and Reason

The substance and spirit of the NRC report were significant in other ways, too. One senses early on, for example, undertones of an adaptive rather than a rigid approach to defining scientific research in education. Thus, adapting the six "guiding principles" that the committee argued were generic across all scientific inquiry to education research—and in particular to the difficult task of identifying whether a particular study or program of study is properly classified as scientific—requires a process of thoughtful deliberation. There is no quick fix here, no algorithm in which to plug the abstract of any given piece of scholarship to test its scientificness. The committee fundamentally rejected such a "dipstick" approach in favor of a more fine-tuned and situation-dependent analysis. "Each field [including education] has features that influence what questions are asked, how research is designed, how it is carried out, and how it is interpreted and generalized. Scholars working in a particular area establish the traditions and standards for how to most appropriately apply the guiding principles to their area of study."[19] The rational approach to identifying whether a program of research is scientific must therefore emphasize thoughtful deliberation; it is the process of making the determination that matters most.

Among the specific features of education that necessitate a careful adaptation of the broad guiding principles, a few stand out for their relevance to this discussion of the procedural rationality of education policy. For example, because education so powerfully evokes conceptions of social value—"people's views about individual human potential, their hopes and expectations of what society can become, and their ideas about how social problems can be alleviated"[50]—the choice of outcomes to study is often as complex as devising measures to assess those outcomes. The problem of outcomes not only poses a constraint on the decisions of individual researchers but also affects the design of reforms and policies at the state and national levels. To the extent that these policy decisions are fluid because of their inherently political origins, even if outcomes are defined for a given study, there is no guarantee (and, indeed, substantial reason to doubt) that those outcomes will be stable long enough to maintain the relevance of research results. This barrier to objectively rational research has been understood for a long time, dating at least to the early movement to establish national indicators of educational progress. (Indeed, one of the problems that continues to plague the National Assessment of Educational Progress is the incongruence of trend analysis with evolving definitions of educational outcomes.)

Perhaps the most relevant of the NRC committee's findings to this discussion of the procedural rationality of scientific research concerns the validity of the so-called gold-standard argument: simply put, it has become fashionable to assert that randomized controlled experimentation is the best way to evaluate the effectiveness of various treatments or interventions. The good news about this rhetoric—introduced by the framers of the new scientifically based research legislation and bolstered by such recent successes as the Tennessee STAR experiment on class-size reduction—is that it placed education research on the same plane as the medical and biological sciences, for which randomization and controlled experimentation have long been staples of the laboratory.[51] Granted, the rhetoric often began with the negative. "Why can't education research be more like medicine?" But for optimists who have long hoped to see education research treated more respectfully, the comparison with medical science was a promising start.

The mixed news about this adventure in the rhetoric of science is that neither the opposition to randomization in education nor the overzealous cheering for such methods in the medical sciences is warranted. There are certainly enough examples of well-structured and carefully administered experimental trials in the behavioral and social sciences; an increasingly sophisticated literature on sources of error and how to manage unforeseen biases in such studies; growing sensitivity on the part of researchers and funders to potential risks of ethical misconduct, especially in studies involving children; and experience in techniques aimed at minimizing those risks. With respect to the use of controlled experimentation in the medical and physical sciences, it is important not to overstate the case. After all, astrophysics research on the movement of the planets and the origins of the universe does not require the establishment of control groups to test major, scientifically defensible hypotheses. Similarly, many of the significant advances in public health are backed not by experiments (there have been no randomized trials involving humans on the effects of tobacco smoke on cancer and other diseases, for example) but by rigorous epidemiological studies involving statistical models designed to reduce (if not eliminate entirely) various types of bias; and the fact that randomized trials have been important in evaluating smoking-cessation programs does not undermine the more general point about the validity of multiple scientific methods. In a word, the rhetoric of "gold standard" does not itself rest on a particularly sturdy evidentiary base.

The bad news about the gold-standard argument is that it can have the perverse effect of narrowing scientific research in education rather than strengthening it. As Paul Holland has noted, "Not all questions are causal."[52] Or, as the NRC report elaborated, there are at least three legitimate types of research questions that are amenable to scientific analysis: (1) what is happening (i.e., accurate descriptions of population characteristics, school conditions, trends in achievement, etc.); (2) what causes things to happen (i.e., does action x cause outcome y?); and (3) how do things happen (i.e., what mechanism or process underlies the observed outcome y caused by action x?). It would be a tragic (and presumably unintended) result if the push for more scientific research in education crowded out the immensely important work of historians, ethnographers, and even statisticians whose studies provide a crucial foundation for understanding where schools are and where they seem to be going—even if this knowledge does not emerge from randomized controlled trials.

At the risk of overstating the case, excessive adherence to the rhetoric of a gold standard can have another perverse effect that relates to the theory of rationality I have been advancing. Not only does reliance on any single method narrow the field of vision necessary for good science, but it also tends to exaggerate the perceived accuracy of the findings. It would be quite understandable if policymakers, parents, teachers, and other decisionmakers assumed that a method hailed for its superiority and for its similarity to methods used by scientists in white lab coats would yield precise answers. It would be natural for the gold-standard rhetoric to mislead the public into believing that such research—and only such research—provides definitive answers to complex questions. Furthermore, this misconception could erode support for programs that have not (yet) gained the credibility that can come only from experimental randomized trials. Raising the bar too high can bring an end to high-jump competition if even the best jumpers can't get over it. Clearly, these effects are worth pondering if one assumes that most education problems are too complex for single best solutions and that what is needed is appropriate deliberation and reasonably good strategies for continuous improvement. Taking explicit account of the fact that education choices are inherently value laden and constrained by strong and legitimate democratic instincts, deliberation over school reform will always necessitate the integration of formal research-based knowledge with the beliefs and wants of the citizenry.

A final observation about the substance and process of scientifically based research. The debate about the scientific nature of education research—and the scientific quality of that research—is certainly not new. There has always been ambivalence in the education research community over the idea that education is or can be a science. Skepticism surrounding the importation of research principles from scientific disciplines—what Ellen Lagemann and others refer to as "physics envy"—has long been a powerful constraint on the development of a bona fide education-research discipline. "A chorus of complaints arose from faculty in the arts and sciences concerning the inclusion of scholars intending to systematically study the organizational and pedagogical aspects of schooling . . . [but] the enterprise grew [nevertheless]," despite internal squabbling and lack of public (federal) research support.[53]

I end this discussion with the following question: Can the reticence among some education researchers to be called scientists explain the delay in extending relevant lessons from cognitive psychology to the realm of education policy and governance? The argument that education is more than science as conventionally imagined gathers strength from the integration of a strand of science on which this book has focused. Cognitive psychology, and the "science of rationality" especially, is based on an inherent appreciation of the intuitive, practical, cultural, and experiential aspects of teaching and learning. At the risk of oversimplification, if behaviorism and the more mechanical theories associated with Thorndike and others have always been distasteful to educators favoring a more humanistic approach, the new science of cognition might be more palatable.[54] Turning this rhetoric into a new (and testable) theory of policy and practice is the task awaiting me in the third and final chapter.

CHAPTER 3

◧

Tinkering toward Rationality

If there is a crisis in American schooling it is not the crisis of putative mediocrity and decline charged by . . . recent reports, but rather the crisis inherent in balancing this tremendous variety of challenges Americans have made on their schools and colleges.

Lawrence Cremin, Popular Education
and Its Discontents, *1990*

Moderation . . .

Aslaksen, in Henrik Ibsen's
An Enemy of the People, *1882*

In their contemplation of the fits and starts of school reform in the twentieth century, historians Larry Cuban and David Tyack make a plea for moderation: "Policy talk about educational reform has been replete with extravagant claims for innovations that flickered and faded. This is a pie-in-the-sky brand of utopianism, and it has often led to disillusionment among teachers and to public cynicism. Exaggeration has pervaded these public rituals of dismay and promise."[1] Following in the tradition of Cremin, Kaestle, Lagemann, Katz, Labaree, Tyack, Lowe, Hansot, Ravitch, and other historians of American education,[2] Tyack and Cuban chronicle the extraordinary experiment in American schooling and dismiss handily the simplistic extremes that permeate public discourse on the quality of teachers, the achievement of kids, and the functioning of the bureaucracy.

Theirs is a call for reason and reasonableness. And as history, their book is richly empirical, their cautionary tale compelling. But it begs the question: Why should a profession steeped in norms of rational discourse and the life of the mind need to be steered back—sometimes kicking and screaming—toward rationality? Why are public expectations for education reform so easily tempted by extreme and grandiose goals? *Why doesn't reasonableness come naturally?*[3]

Tyack and Cuban lay the crucial groundwork but do not answer the question; history describes but it does not explain.[4] At the risk of stretching an already tired cliché, what is needed in addition to the chronicling of the often bizarre rhetorical and substantive character of education reform is a theory of action, a framework that connects observation to prediction and lays a foundation for reasonable program and policy goals.

What should be included in a theory to explain observed education policies that seem to escape rational judgment? How might such a theory provide a basis for the design of more rational policies in the future? In a sense, these questions have motivated this book, and it may be helpful here to review the basic logic, especially with Tyack and Cuban's history as backdrop. First, although the question about reasonableness in education reform is intuitively appealing, it implies an embedded definition of rationality that is out of place. Most people would like to believe in an idealized vision of solutions to our educational problems and, implicitly at least, apply a kind of objective-rationality criterion to their assessment of successes and failures of various reform strategies. In our mind's eye exists some kind of optimal answer . . . and no one really wants to think that cataracts blur that vision. Selecting the best course of action from a complete and readily accessible list of options is nice as a stylized textbook model of psychological functioning but not relevant to most of the interesting decisions people really face. Second, it is the joining of truly complex problems with the cognitive bounds on human problem solving that forces a new approach to defining rationality, one which emphasizes the sensibility of *process* as much as (or even more than) the after-the-fact measurement of the "rightness" of any particular answer. This is, indeed, the notion of procedural rationality, the linchpin of what may be viewed as a campaign to restore reasonableness in both the rhetoric and practice of education policy.

But first, a brief digression to handle two anticipated worries. To the extent that procedural rationality builds from the assumption of limited human information-processing capacity (i.e., *bounded* rationality), some may suspect that I am tolerating, if not advancing, an erosion of standards. Is the admission of bounded rationality a lazy way out of seeking answers to tough problems? Does it imply surrender to the forces of whim, religion, and impulse?[5] Does it mean that I advocate more "blink" and less think?[6] The answer to each of these questions is the same: no. There is nothing substandard about the awareness that most interesting problems in the world defy optimal solutions, and that people frequently make decisions in spite of the daunting complexity and uncertainty which obscures the potential consequences of their actions. Rather, I submit that the persistent *denial* of complexity does more to undermine the discovery of good solutions than would the unembarrassed expression of humility and the honest articulation of reasonable goals and timetables.

The denial of complexity is usually tacit more than explicit, and it often is camouflaged in the gripping rhetoric of impending moral or economic demise. At times it is literally a call to arms, as in the famous phrasing of *A Nation at Risk:* "If an unfriendly foreign power had attempted to impose on America the mediocre educational performance that exists today, we might well have viewed it as an act of war," which is then followed by comforting palliatives about pragmatic problem solving and national fortitude as the path to redemption. Denial of complexity and bounds to human decision-making capacity fuels the seemingly addictive cycle of immodest hyperbole in both the description of current conditions and the prescription of remedies; exaggerated claims and the specter of emergency lead to grandiose expectations followed by disappointment, demoralization, and, ultimately, inertia.

Taking this pernicious logic one step farther, it is not hard to see how overpromising can unintentionally lead to an erosion of confidence and reduction of support for rigorous analysis. If government agencies that support scientific research are embarrassed by disappointing results—an almost inevitable consequence of setting goals too high in the first place—they may encounter increased pressure from those who distrust scientific inquiry altogether. In a word, if expensive science cannot deliver the goods, why not return to a more intuitive, humanistic, even religious basis for solving tough problems?[7]

Worse yet, the cycle of exuberance and gloom can have a frustratingly self-fulfilling quality. Almost as if they anticipate the inevitable disappointment that arises from unfulfilled goals, many otherwise thoughtful and well-meaning people assume a priori that progress in human affairs is unlikely, if not impossible. The fear of failure, coupled with the natural (and healthy) tendency to look for weak links in chains of causal reasoning, leads to the expression of doubt and suspicion *even when early evidence suggests that a program is achieving desired results.*

As Albert Hirschman has shown, this tendency used to be associated with right-wing opposition to social programs, but it is now more evenly distributed across the ideological spectrum: leftists often have trouble accepting evidence of anything good emanating from a conservative administration they palpably despise. On one hand, it is in the nature of scientists to be skeptical, and I am certainly not advocating casual acceptance of untested claims or the adoption of intervention strategies without any evidence for their potential effects. My concern is about what happens if skepticism is allowed to drown out progress—that is, if it turns into an undisciplined methodological nihilism in which *no* findings are tolerated except those that point to flaws in proposed policies and practices. The importance of this hazard cannot be overestimated, and its basis as an argument for renewed attention to appropriate evidentiary standards in education (and, more broadly, social-science) research cannot be overemphasized.[8]

If, on the other hand, scientific inquiry is understood as an incremental process of knowledge accumulation involving the combination of multiple types of data, rather than a single method that promises definitive answers to well-defined causal questions, the likelihood of dramatic swings of exuberance and despair may be reduced and the attractiveness of political attacks on science may be rendered less defensible. It may seem counterintuitive, but my argument is that *science is furthered, not hindered, by the acknowledgment of complexity and the admission of bounded human problem-solving capacity.*

The second concern that I need to address, regarding procedural rationality, relates to a distinction made in the literature of moral philosophy and especially the theory of justice.[9] In my usage, procedural rationality means something like practicality, or pragmatism, or doing the smartest thing possible under the very real constraints of time, resources, and context. It is about practical feasibility, or what Simon called "computational feasibility," so that, for example, "crunching the numbers" to list out and compare all possible moves and outcomes in a chess game might be objectively or substantively rational but clearly infeasible procedurally. (After all, serious chess matches are timed events.)

This meaning of procedural rationality is different, however, from the way philosophers might think about the correctness of outcomes as a function purely of the fairness of the process that produces them. For example, given two otherwise equally qualified individuals, a coin toss might be a procedurally acceptable way to ensure fairness; and disagreement about the result would, necessarily, focus on the validity of the process (was the coin weighted, did it bounce properly, etc.). In John Rawls's philosophy, perhaps the most significant contribution to justice theory of the past century, it is even possible to distinguish perfect procedural justice from imperfect procedural justice: the former implies both a process and an outcome that are pure.[10]

My interest in procedural rationality, then, is clearly not meant to suggest that *if a process seems appropriate then whatever solution emerges is the rational one.* Where I have suggested, for example, that Americans' preference for a complex school system still primarily governed through public rather than private choices suggests a certain kind of collective procedural rationality, the intent is not that the outcome thereby becomes immune from further critique or correction. Even if the democratic processes that get us our schools are, at least comparatively speaking, fair, that does not guarantee the results are what we would always feel comfortable calling rational. Rather, my point is that we citizens and other participants in the hodgepodge of American education policy have a more or less inchoate sense of how we'd like our kids taught—here again, think about Aristotle's dictum that people "inevitably differ in their conceptions of the good life, and hence they will inevitably disagree on matters of education"[11]—and that the system we have meets enough of those objectives closely enough so that, warts and all, we tend to go along with it. The very fact that we believe in the virtue of the hodgepodge, a necessary condition in our uniquely heterogeneous and antiauthoritarian style of democracy, makes likely the acceptance—at least temporarily—of suboptimal educational outcomes.

But the absence of an optimum clearly does not diminish the pursuit of better and better outcomes, through debate and experimentation and continued trial and error.[12]

I end this digression on two notes. First, my preference for reasonableness certainly does *not* simplify matters. It makes the task of education-policy thinking and evaluation more difficult. If the appeal to moderation is intuitively appealing, it is not easy to translate into measures and benchmarks that are the currency of public accountability and political action. Second, I shall restate a central hypothesis of these papers: a theory based on principles of procedural rationality can explain—and one hopes alleviate—the problem of failed expectations in education policy and the problem of evidentiary standards in education research. To extend the metaphor introduced by Tyack and Cuban, my goal here is to show that there is more hope in tinkering toward rationality than in tinkering toward utopia. I begin this chapter by revisiting the concept of procedural rationality and how it relates to education-policy choices and the ways they are understood and articulated. The discussion is motivated by recent reporting in the mainstream press on the complexities of research about how to teach science in the lower grades.

I then contrast the procedural approach to the more conventional production function that underlies much economic research on the organization of schools and the costs and benefits of education-policy choices. There are clearly other frameworks represented in the literature of school organization and policy, but I am primarily interested in emulating for education the success that a cognitively inspired alternative theory has enjoyed in other domains.[13]

Finally, I will recommend steps to make education policy and rhetoric more procedurally rational. The key feature of my proposed compact—viewed perhaps as an implicit "memorandum of understanding" between researchers and policymakers—is an agreement to ratchet down the rhetoric of reform, *but not too much*. The challenge is to imagine a thermostat—and to adjust it enough to restore the possibility for reasonable expectations and reduced like-lihood of disappointment, but not so much as to squelch idealism and its importance in motivating social progress. The fact that no such thermostat currently exists—and that it is unclear where in our complex and cherished democracy we would install one even if we could design it—should be a source of comfort to those who thought I was going to venture an optimal solution to the questions I have raised.

PROCEDURAL RATIONALITY
AND THE PERVERSITY OF STANDARDS

A recent story in the *Wall Street Journal* demonstrates that maximi-zation assumptions are deeply entrenched in Western culture, even if human decisionmakers rarely enjoy the luxury of facing prob-lems for which the search for optimal answers could be called ratio-nal. "The *Best* Ways to Make Schoolchildren Learn? We Just Don't *Know*," announces the headline under the banner "Science Jour-nal."[14] The syntax is revealing (I have italicized key words to make the point), the tone suggestive of a latent schadenfreude common in so many popular and professional commentaries about the limits of science. To assume that any proposal to improve student learning would ever meet the stringent criteria implied by the word "best" is, at minimum (!), highly doubtful. The barriers are perhaps obvi-ous: What is meant by learning? Will the measure chosen to evalu-ate the learning be valid, reliable, stable, and robust across diverse populations? Does the question imply *all* schoolchildren learning *maximally?* Or would it be enough if *some* children learned *some-thing?* And if the measurement problems are not sufficiently daunt-ing, there is a raft of political, ethical, and values questions that complicate matters further. Some may ask, Whose right is it, any-way, to make children do anything?

At the risk of turning a rather banal journalistic question into a Talmudic exegesis—or worse, a nightmare of postmodern deconstruction—I would offer the perhaps equally banal answer that neither the usage of "best" nor the implied meaning of "know" (which I take here to mean "know with certitude") are well suited to the complex problems of education and the limited computational capacity of educators.[15] Once again, if even something conceptually simple, like the traveling-salesman problem—in which the outcome is clearly defined, the relevant data are readily at hand, and there are no apparent ethical quandaries—eludes "best" solutions, does it not follow that "the *best* ways" to educate is a strange oxymoron? Put differently, why does procedural rationality seem to come naturally to people coping with situations such as the traveling-salesman problem but less so in cases involving even more complex and ill-defined problems, such as the improvement of learning and the expansion of educational opportunities to the masses?

Indeed, the *Wall Street Journal* article does a better job than its headline in teasing apart the complexities of teaching, and it unintentionally lays out a persuasive rationale for moderation in defining expectations for student learning. Here is the crux of the story as reported: "It is conventional wisdom . . . that the *best way* to give K–12 students a deep and enduring understanding is through 'discovery learning' . . . [a] term [that] has no precise, universally accepted definition" (italics added). Research into this ill-defined but quite widely accepted proposition by one of the best cognitive psychologists/education researchers yielded an answer that is no doubt disappointing to at least some people: " 'I'm not saying kids *never* benefit from discovering something on their own,' says Professor [David] Klahr. 'But especially for complicated, multi-step procedures, there are just no data that discovery learning offers *any* benefit' " (italics added). So Klahr concedes that some kids may in fact benefit (compared with what or whom is not included in the *Jour-*

nal's summary of Klahr's research), but then even he slides into a less moderate (and somewhat contradictory) warning that there's no evidence of *any* benefits!

My point here is not to catch Klahr or the *Wall Street Journal* in a semantic trap but to suggest that both Klahr's research and the newspaper story about it offer compelling testimony on behalf of something other than a maximizing framework in which to understand education. Perhaps the most important lesson to ponder from the headline, the story, and the more detailed facts of the subject research is this: science educators and researchers studying science education may dream about optimal solutions, but in reality they behave more modestly, looking for and settling for evidence that may not offer the definitive answer but at least propels both teaching and the study of teaching in arguably promising directions. *Summarizing* that behavior, however, in a newspaper story or other format, means abridging the details and nuances, which sometimes creates the impression of idealized expectations and inevitable frustration. Ironically, it is the procedural rationality of good journalism—providing reasonably good and well-founded approximations of complex phenomena for wide audiences with widely disparate levels of expertise—that perpetuates the impression of a system that is, on the whole, glued to an optimizing mentality in constant pursuit of maximal solutions.

More than a curious rhetorical puzzle, the problem of describing complex decision processes in parsimonious and understandable language suggests several core axioms for a framework designed to bring order and reasonableness to the apparent chaos of education policy. First, evidence of continued ambiguity over effects of alternative teaching methods or curricula is not sufficient to infer zero gains in knowledge from research. It is perhaps frustrating to lay readers, but entirely acceptable to honest scientists, that conclusions from an experiment or program of study leave large numbers of questions unanswered and render some issues only partially resolved.[16] Fortunately, however, the slow march of scholarship occasionally reaches a point in the journey at which a preponderance of evidence provides a compelling and defensible rationale for certain courses of action—and against certain other courses of action.[17]

Second, the obvious preference among researchers for evidence that a given system of curriculum and pedagogy "works" should not be construed necessarily as a lack of humility or an impatience with the slow pace and incremental quality of scholarship. On the surface, there is some rather blatant hubris in employing language that smacks of grandiose or utopian expectations—that is, that creates the impression that good research will reveal, once and for all, how to teach reading to any and all children. But it pays to consider a more charitable assumption: perhaps the proponents of this brand of rhetoric understand the need for some hyperbole, some extremism, to fuel the engine of change and that, in fact, they will be delighted to settle for more moderate results. My favorite example of rhetoric that exceeded the underlying empirical evidence is *A Nation at Risk.* The question I am raising here is whether the benefits of spurring a generation of public and private attention to educational improvement justify the compromise to research fidelity and scientific purity. Is the implicit acceptance of high-pitched rhetoric itself an example of compromise and procedural rationality?

Who is more rational—the proponent of idealized rhetoric who understands it is a necessary means toward an acceptable end and is willing (within limits) to risk cyclical disappointment and demoralization? Or the skeptic who knows that lofty goals are unattainable and resists efforts that compromise standards of empirical inquiry? There is no clear answer to this question (its complexity rules out an optimal answer . . .), but it points to the importance of confronting (and, one hopes, reducing) the potentially perverse effects of radical goals and unrealistically high standards of evidence. I shall return to these issues in my discussion of a new compact between researchers and policymakers.

BEYOND PRODUCTION

I began this book with a reasonably simple observation: cognitive science has revolutionized the theory of teaching and learning and paved the way to new theories of organization, but it has had little or no effect on theories of schools and school systems as organizations. (I have since amended the basic formulation to encompass the rhetorical side of policy: theories of rationality can also contribute to greater understanding of the origins and effects of the hyperbole that surrounds much education policy and research.)

In the economic theory of organization, cognitive principles alter the nature of assumptions and predictions in fundamental ways. Rather than assume that firms *maximize* profit and that individuals *maximize* utility, the alternative model assumes that economic actors have bounded rationality and settle for reasonably good solutions (rather than pursue objective optima) to complex problems. In the language proposed by Simon, they "satisfice." Can this variation on the conventional economic model illuminate problems and strategies in education? A brief digression to review the principles of the neoclassical (maximizing) and cognitive (satisficing) models is in order. As a reminder, I focus here on economic theories of the firm not because they are the only (or best) way to model the organization of education but because their impact on other fields— such as deregulation, antitrust, firm-sponsored training, and the provision of public goods—may be exportable to school reform and related issues.

The architecture of the conventional theory of economic organization is the production function, a positive predictive model in which the validity of assumptions is less important than the purported reliability of its predictions.[18] In the case of a manufacturing firm, for example, what concerns the economic theorist is not the intricacies of internal organization but rather its output. Regardless of its lack of face validity, the assumption that managers convert inputs to finished products in order to maximize profit provides the basis for a number of useful predictions, such as on the relationship between productivity and wages and the relationship between market prices and quantity of goods produced. What goes on inside the black box—that is, the details of organizational design or the effects of production technology on worker productivity—is of limited interest; those issues are finessed largely by the assumption of technical efficiency—that is, that a given quantity of outputs cannot be produced with fewer inputs. What remains is the question of allocative efficiency—that is, whether firms produce quantities of goods that will maximize returns in a competitive market. Productivity is therefore defined simply as output per unit of labor, and orthodox neoclassical economists happily cede to their friends in the business school most considerations of management and organization.[19]

Among the virtues of the neoclassical model is its reliance on relatively few and easily observed variables. Prices and quantities of inputs are assumed measurable, prices of finished products are determined by competitive market forces, and the central problem is to estimate quantities of output that maximize the difference between revenues and costs. Identification of the mathematical form of the production function and reliable estimation of coefficients on the factors of production are empirical challenges, but the underlying model is tantalizing in its parsimony, its appeal to beliefs about the purposefulness of human behavior, its idealized and very complimentary assumption about human problem-solving capacity, and its wonderfully simplified assumption that transactions are costless.[20] Note that in the conventional theory of the firm, the basic unit of analysis—the firm—is taken as a datum. Why transactions are organized through structures called firms, of varying size and character, is not on the table. Only the estimation of the firm's productive output is of interest, assuming the goal of profit maximization under competitive market conditions, exogenously determined prices of production factors, and perfect information on the part of managers.

The cognitively inspired alternative has a number of variants that go under the general rubric of a *behavioral* theory of the firm,[21] which propose a number of crucial amendments to the input-output character of the neoclassical vision. First, managers are not assumed to be omniscient with respect to competitive conditions. Rather, they are visualized as decisionmakers with bounded rationality facing complex external conditions, and their goal is to make reasonably good choices rather than seek objective optima. They are not expected to have the information, time, or knowledge to *maximize* anything, any more than the traveling salesman is assumed to pursue the perfect answer to complex problems requiring inordinate computational capacity and unlimited time in which to act. Prediction is still the focus in the behavioral theory—even though significantly greater attention is paid to the context of decisionmaking, opportunities for adaptive corrections based on assessment of multiple streams of information, and the likely possibility that rational managers will accept second- or third-best strategies rather than hold out for empirically verifiable optima.

According to proponents of this approach, taking behavior seriously really means explicitly accounting for the effects of thought on action and exploring the effects of organizational relationships on how information is processed and inputs are converted to outputs. It requires the willingness to peer inside the black box of production, which, it is hoped, will enable better predictions and more useful explanations than the standard input-output models. It is worth noting that behavioral economists do not in any way downgrade the value of prediction as the gold standard of a theory's validity, but they argue, rather, that improving the validity of assumptions with cognitive and social nuance enhances not only the believability of the model but its predictive validity as well.

At the core of behavioral theories of the firm lies an inherent acceptance of procedural, rather than objective, rationality. Managers are assumed to have limited information-processing capacity and limited knowledge of the forces affecting market conditions. In a sense, they are assumed to be more humble—and therefore more willing to make decisions based on partial data, as long as those decisions follow a reasonable amount of thoughtful deliberation. The neoclassical model, by comparison, hinges on assumptions of perfect information and the pursuit of idealized optimal answers: profit maximization, utility maximization, and cost minimization are coins in the neoclassical realm.

In education, it might seem obvious that conditions are not hospitable to the maximizers. Outcomes are poorly defined and subject to considerable ideological and emotional swings; student mobility limits the accuracy of data collection; the canons of knowledge change; and in democratic environments priorities shift and educators are expected to keep up with the seemingly endless parade of innovations, all promising substantially accelerated and widespread achievement. Nevertheless, the production-function model has withstood many attacks, and, despite occasionally powerful contestations from researchers who are willing to challenge underlying assumptions, it continues to provide a compelling—albeit depressing—framework for explaining and dictating education policy.[22]

The basic model posits that an educational outcome, such as academic achievement, is a function of various inputs, such as expenditures on school resources, the quality of teachers, and an array of student background variables, including family income, parents' educational attainment, and neighborhood (geographic) variables. The key question is reduced to one with obvious appeal for policymaking: By how much can achievement be expected to increase for marginal increases in any of the inputs? The model is unfairly accused of insinuating an assembly-line image of education, when it is in fact highly stylized to enable predictions of change in outcome for changes in input.[23] And even the most creative economists willing to entertain deviations from the standard production function acknowledge its importance in addressing many of the questions that policymakers and the public seem determined to ask.

Not surprisingly, the finding that changes in resources (as measured by expenditures) are not associated with replicable and meaningful gains in student achievement (as measured by test scores) has provoked several decades of controversy and frustration. At its worst, the model has been responsible for reducing the complexities of education and school reform policy to a seemingly silly question ("Does money matter?"[24]), although recent efforts to unpack the business of *how* resources are expended have yielded some progress both in terms of understanding the processes of teaching and learning and in terms of developing more interesting theories of education. One feature of this line of research is the implicit rejection of technical efficiency and a determination to explore the details of how resources are utilized by decisionmakers in complex educational settings; those pursuing this strand, however, are typically not economists, so they are not burdened by any allegiance to the underlying production function.

Fortunately, a handful of economists have been willing to challenge neoclassical assumptions as they relate to education, but they have made only modest progress toward a robust alternative that offers as much methodological efficiency and predictive validity. Most notably, Richard Murnane and Richard Nelson have articulated a general argument for analyzing productivity and the adoption of innovation when the underlying techniques—in the case of education, the skills of teaching and learning—are tacit rather than explicit. The notion of tacit knowledge comes from Michael Polanyi, who noticed that many activities require know-how that cannot easily be articulated and transformed into clear action principles or algorithmic rules. For Polanyi, the classical example is bicycle riding: you don't learn it by studying a manual but rather by doing it, and those who do it best are not necessarily (and are often the least likely to be) able to write out what they are doing in language that is effective in teaching the skill to others.[25]

Cognitive science has made significant contributions to the evolution of expertise, which frequently involves the mastery of skills by people not necessarily inclined toward eloquent verbal explanations of what they are doing.[26] One can only imagine if Yogi Berra were a model not of *catching* a baseball but of *explaining how he does it!* Tacit knowledge, therefore, evokes a specific form of bounded rationality, the limited capability of people to explain (to themselves or others) how they do certain tasks. (It is interesting to note that the tasks do not need to be complex: after all, bicycle riding is not complex in any objective sense, but only in terms of how difficult it is to capture and communicate its essence clearly.) Without such capacity, standards of performance are difficult if not impossible to articulate in advance, which renders the task of accountability particularly onerous, especially if fairness and transparency are valued.[27]

From the standpoint of production theory, the assumption of tacit skills substantially complicates the use of conventional variables, such as teachers' educational attainment (input) or students' performance on standardized tests (output). In the Murnane and Nelson formulation, techniques and inputs (curriculum, teaching) evolve rather than being rationally chosen, and production is viewed as a continually adaptive effort to solve problems; classroom life is seen as a vibrant arena for experimentation in which teachers and learners must try strategies and revise them as they go, rather than as a smoothly running routine in which laboratory-proven methods can be applied uniformly and with homogeneous results. There is no autopilot option in most classrooms, and even the most sophisticated computer-assisted instructional systems depend on judgment and rapid adjustment by teachers. (In fact, the more sophisticated the technology, the *more* it is intended to supplement rather than supplant human interactions.)[28]

Without the illusion of routine, the robustness and generalizability of even a well-identified production function deteriorates rapidly. In the lingo of statistical methodology, the "external validity" of just about any pedagogical or curricular strategy is limited. Production-function enthusiasts who are not persuaded by arguments to increase spending on education derive a certain sadistic pleasure from demonstrating that what works in one classroom with one group of students does not easily transfer even to other classrooms in the same building, let alone to other schools or districts or countries. But the result is less surprising to those who assume something other than a stable and controllable production system. As Murnane and Nelson note, "In particular, techniques or programs found to be successful in an original site have, with monotonous regularity, not had the same effect in other sites. Often performance in the original site has failed to be maintained. The proximate explanation for the inability to replicate successes is clear: the same curricula and instructional strategies are used in different ways in different sites."[29]

The assumption of idiosyncrasy rather than routine in techniques of production evokes themes that I hope are by now familiar. Without a stable and tangible definition of output and a consistent technology to produce it, the notion of maximization clearly loses meaning. *We are again in the realm of procedure—that is, the effective management of decisions that require adaptation, flexibility, and reaction to unanticipated stimuli.* More complex even than the traveling-salesman problem, in which both the outcome and the computational technology are known (but the information-processing time is overwhelming), educational production is plagued by ill-defined goals and imprecise technologies that do not replicate easily across classrooms, students, or schools.

The problem, of course, is that understanding the limitations of conventional theory for handling production when techniques are tacit, though necessary, is not sufficient for developing a good alternative theory—or at least one that would be robust enough to dislodge the neoclassical paradigm. And it is not as though such a shift would be unwelcome to a frustrated scholarly community that rues the extent to which the conventional paradigm dominates economic research, "despite the fact that its use has greater potential for obfuscation than elucidation."[30]

One promising avenue for improved theory would build on the foundations of the "new institutional economics," a body of rigorous economic theory with significant implications for the organization and governance of complex transactions. Idiosyncrasy in production, for example, is a key assumption in Oliver Williamson's organizational-failures framework, which I described briefly in chapter 2 and to which I now pay a return visit. It is a comprehensive model that accounts explicitly for bounded rationality, environmental complexity, and the effects of opportunistic self-interest seeking on the part of participants in economic and social transactions. The model departs from the neoclassical tradition in several significant ways. It dismisses the fiction of perfect information and zero transaction costs in economic activity, assumes rather a set of behavioral limits (and human traits, such as opportunism and "self-interest seeking with guile") coupled with uncertainties inherent in complex decisions, and is concerned primarily with the effects of idiosyncratic rather than routine modes of production. Rather than taking firms or other hierarchical organizations as given, Williamson proposes that they exist (in different forms) because they enable sequential and adaptive decisions needed to cope with and govern complex transactions. Whereas some transactions are best handled through atomistic competition and the execution of implicit spot contracts, situations with nonroutine decisions and imperfect information (i.e., most of the interesting ones in the modern age) require collective or hierarchical governance that would not be necessary in perfectly competitive environments.

Where Murnane and Nelson pause in their development of a cognitively anchored theory of educational production, Ernest House continues with a direct application of the Williamson framework.[31] House's entry into this arena is commendable especially because he is not an economist; he turned this deficit to significant advantage by drilling through some of the complex syntax of transactions-cost economics and allowing some new light to shine on basic principles of educational policy and evaluation.

The focus in House's paper and book on this topic is on three of the pillars in Williamson's framework—namely, bounded rationality, opportunism, and asset specificity. The first of these I have belabored sufficiently. Opportunism is defined (by Williamson) as "self-interest seeking with guile," a lovely locution that captures a wide range of behaviors in which individuals use information strategically for their own advantage; these behaviors can be said to push the notion of self-interest in the direction of an imagined ethical frontier—without necessarily crossing it. A good example is the consumer in an insurance market who is asked to disclose relevant information about prior driving behavior. How much does such a person disclose with complete truthfulness? (A perhaps familiar educational example would be the tendency on the part of students to withhold evidence that their parents played a significant role in completing a science-fair entry.)

Notably, the limits to full disclosure are not entirely strategic: there are many situations in which even the most ethically bound individuals forget or are unable to articulate key aspects of their behavior in any meaningful way. The combined effect of opportunism and the constraints of tacit knowledge (what Williamson refers to as "information impactedness" i.e., the difficulty people have remembering and expressing accurately information that might be relevant to given transactions) creates barriers to the efficient functioning of markets and leads to nonmarket modes of organizing those transactions. The third element in the Williamson framework that House considers, asset specificity, is about the efficiency of market transactions when assets are not easily transferred. People who invest in financial resources can usually trade them in standard markets. But when people invest in (or acquire) assets that do not transfer, such as skills that are highly specific to an idiosyncratic job, the value of the asset and the governance of transactions involving the asset are problematic. As House notes, in conventional market theory "faceless buyers and sellers meet to exchange standardized goods at equilibrium prices . . . [while] in asset-specific situations the identify of the person with whom one is doing business does matter."[32]

From these core concepts, House proposes a novel and potentially useful approach to evaluating the attributes of educational reforms. He gives the framers of national educational goals, for example, zeroes in the bounded rationality and opportunism categories, because those issues were not sufficiently considered in the design and implementation of the policy. In retrospect, accounting for the likelihood that teachers might attempt to "game" standardized tests because of opportunistic inclinations, and that bounded rationality prevents teachers and administrators from achieving defined goals "even if they wanted to," the Williamson-cum-House model would have predicted some formidable obstacles to the accomplishment of the national-goals policy of the late 1980s.

My purpose in offering these abridged glimpses into two overlapping strategies for thinking about education policy and reform is to suggest the value in paying attention to cognitive variables. Enhancing understanding, however, is not sufficient for promoting improved programs and policies; the description of individual and organizational constraints on objectively rational decisionmaking invites consideration of a normative framework for improved decisions in the future. A first sketch of such a framework is my goal in the final section of this chapter.

A MODERATE PROPOSAL

I shall resist the temptation to offer here a grand theory, even if I thought I had one. Suggesting a framework that neatly ties together the descriptive, evaluative, predictive, and normative functions of research, establishes a formal and practical link between research and policy, and establishes reasonable rhetorical bounds on reform would be immodest, if not hypocritical, especially after all the pleading for moderation that flows through these chapters.

In keeping with my preference for procedural reasonableness over the extravagances of optimality and finality, therefore, I offer here a preliminary set of modest recommendations. They are intended for researchers and policymakers—but should be studied by intermediaries such as think tanks and education journalists too—who are willing to apply principles of procedural rationality to their respective jobs. The proposal is outlined in the form of a compact, an imaginary memorandum of understanding, which, if enforced, might restore some modicum of reasonableness to the continuing debates over how to improve education and how to know if policies and practices are working. I include some illustrative examples (mostly drawn from discussions in this and earlier chapters) in the hope their key features will be generic enough to extend to future problems and situations.

Researchers Should . . .

1. *Adjust their evaluative models and evidentiary standards from an implied criterion of optimality to one that reflects reasonable outcomes in terms of magnitude of improvement and timelines for achieving it.* Although evaluators are frequently called on to collect data and as-

sess progress toward goals defined extravagantly by policymakers (hint: dealing with this problem will be the number-one task of policymakers and the media), the evaluator/research community has a responsibility to sound the alarm of unreasonableness and proactively contain expectations to procedurally rational levels. There is no simple algorithm (yet) for setting levels reasonably, although my proposal here rests on two hopes: (1) that conscious attention to the reasonableness of evaluative criteria may, in and of itself, provide some relief and (2) that efforts to set reasonable targets will gradually become the norm both among researchers and the policymaking community that is responsible for setting goals and implementing reform. (Understanding the role of rhetorical flourish in instigating change and avoiding the perception that researchers are hopelessly negative are key elements of this general recommendation. I address this more in recommendation number 2, below.)

Two examples come to mind. As I suggested in reviewing the debates over test-score linkage, the appropriate question for researchers/evaluators is not simply whether a linkage plan is optimal but, rather, whether such a plan would result in *satisfactory* levels of score validity and reliability for specific intended uses of the results. Put differently, the questions that should guide researchers/evaluators (which I have referred to elsewhere as the "Mosteller challenge") are these: How severe are the risks of degradation to validity? How hazardous are the likely errors in inferences about linked scores? Are these downside risks tolerable in view of anticipated benefits?[33] This approach extends well beyond the narrow problem of linkage and could become the focus of discussion surrounding test-based accountability more generally.

The second example concerns the No Child Left Behind Act. It is not sufficient to note that currently articulated goals are unreasonable, although that is certainly an appropriate—and scientifically ethical—necessary step. There is no doubt that a federal law (program) with such broad and powerful intended effects requires serious attention to assumed capacities and baseline conditions of schools and students.[34] However, those researchers accepting procedural rationality as the guiding framework should consider four amendments to their normal mode of operations.

First, they should explore *the extent to which* the stated goals will fall short, according to various estimates or assumptions of pace of achievement gain, during the legislated time period. Second, they might consider a model that estimates the marginal likelihood of achieving the goals (or coming close) for small increments of additional time. In other words, if the goals in NCLB are not likely to be attained by 2014 under current assumptions of resource expenditures, how much more money would it take? Third, they should examine the counterfactual argument—that is, whether in the absence of the accountability policy of the No Child Left Behind Act and its combination of rewards and sanctions, the predictable growth or stagnation in achievement gain would be acceptable. Finally, they should try to recognize the benefits and hazards of the existing rhetorical aspects of the program (i.e., its obvious grandiosity) and weigh those benefits and hazards against the risks of stagnation in educational improvement that might ensue from a weaker (albeit more realistic) set of stated goals.

2. *Curb their enthusiasm for the "finding fatal flaws" syndrome.* In social science generally (especially economics) and in education policy specifically, the urge to look for potential flaws in policies seems to be an involuntary reflex. How can researchers be faithful to the scientific quest for objectivity and at the same time sensitive to the downside risks associated with premature negativity that erodes morale of reformers and, as Hirschman would warn, harms democratic discourse? The challenge is not trivial: researchers should understand that the validation of programs or practices may have unintended effects on the morale of policymakers and reformers and may slow the pace of innovation and discovery necessary for long-

term progress in the organization of schooling and the improvement of teaching and learning. There is no objectively easy or optimal answer to this question, and the procedurally rational approach
requires (1) a general awareness of the issue and (2) decisions that
are situation specific.

A recent example illustrates the problem. One of the more unpleasant episodes in recent years was the rapid rejection of minor-
ity-student score gains in Texas on grounds of suspected mischief
in the inclusion of students and/or inappropriate coaching prior to
and even during test administration.[35] Granted, there was indeed
evidence of some mischief, and the speed with which minority students' scores had risen was certainly worthy of deeper analysis. But
those who thought they had found the "smoking gun" (teaching to
the test, cheating, other violations of testing procedures) and shout-
ed foul conveyed, unintentionally perhaps, that *if minority kids'
scores go up it must be the result of something other than the possibility
that these kids are actually learning more or becoming better readers.*

Did the schadenfreude that emanated from the researchers who
claimed to have found anomalies arise purely from their instincts
as scientists and their joy at discovering the statistically misleading
quality of observed score gains? Or was it spurred by a more insidi-
ous underlying assumption, namely that poor minority kids are in-
nately unable to become proficient readers? Not wishing to impugn
motives here, I accept the more charitable guess. (This is a safe guess,
based on my personal acquaintance with the researchers involved.
Others may hold different views.) But my concern is that the *effect*
of this reaction on the morale of reading teachers, school reformers,
parents, and the kids themselves must have been painful. How can
the efforts to save minority children from a life of low expectations
and poor performance be sustained in the face of constant suspicion
that any evidence of progress is bogus? It is worth remembering, in
this context, Hirschman's admonition: "As long as the social world
moves at all in response to human action for change, even if in the

wrong direction, hope remains that it can somehow be steered correctly. But the demonstration or discovery that such action is incapable of 'making a dent' at all leaves the promoters of change humiliated, demoralized, in doubt about the meaning and true motive of their endeavors."[36]

Lest there be any doubt, I am not proposing here that researchers suppress unpleasant findings for the sake of protecting certain individuals or groups from the harsh truth of science. The case of New York City, recently again in the news because of disputes over rapid and large score gains, will again test the capacity of our research and policy system to find a reasonable way out. New York parents deserve information that is at least reasonably valid and reliable; reformers who have worked tirelessly to improve the lot of all New York students deserve to be credited for at least some progress, even if not at the levels now reported.[37] In any event, my point is that research findings have consequences because of how they are interpreted and then used to justify policies; it is incumbent on both the producers and users of scientific evidence to consider the intended as well as the unintended inferences that may be made based on analyses of policies or programs.[38] Such consideration is a necessary step toward ensuring that education research is embraced as a valuable tool in the formation of reasonable policies and not eschewed for its inevitable negativity or dismissed for its mischievous irrelevance.

3. *Communicate to intended users whether a study is mainly descriptive or normative and what evidentiary standards should apply in translating the findings into policy or practice.* The arguments about methodology in education research often seem disconnected from the question of use. Does it make sense to call randomized field trials the "gold standard" without specifying how the inferences from a given experiment are germane to a specific policy or practice choice?

Proponents of experimentation in education research tend to take for granted that the main policy problem is the evaluation of programs, before or after they are implemented, for the sake of making better (if not objectively rational) resource-allocation decisions. There is no doubt about the legitimacy of the underlying question: Assuming scarce resources (at the school or district level, for example), does a particular reading (or mathematics or history or . . .) curriculum hold the greatest promise to raise achievement? What is the evidence?

Leaving aside the thorny issue of establishing causality in controlled social experiments,[39] a responsibility of researchers is to indicate a priori where a given study or body of work lies in the ecology of scientific research. Is a given study intended primarily to evaluate the effects of a defined treatment on a set of defined outcomes, to describe complex and inchoate phenomena and explore trends and patterns in data, to propose a solution to a known problem, to guide management choices involving human and financial resources, or to shed new light on familiar problems by focusing on small samples of individuals or schools or other units of analysis?

If step 1 is specifying the nature of a given research project, using perhaps the typology listed above as a first approximation, then step 2 is providing guidance on the utility of the evidence for various types of policy or practice decisions. I do not mean to suggest that researchers are solely responsible for how their findings are used; indeed, such a burden would be both unfair and counterproductive. Rather, I submit that at least some of the confusion over methodology and the utility of education research would be eased if researchers were more explicit about underlying theory and the nature of inferences and about the relationship between findings and warrants for action. Perhaps most important, researchers need to be aware of the almost certain likelihood that their findings will be overinterpreted for political or ideological gain and that the quality of scientific findings is enhanced—not diminished—by honest expression of their limitations.

A recent example illustrates the importance of situating and qualifying education research. David Berliner's address to the 2005 American Educational Research Association, on poverty and achievement, drew a standing ovation from a standing-room-only audience in one of the largest banquet rooms in the Montreal Sheraton. His eloquent review of the overwhelming preponderance of evidence that poverty is the "600-pound gorilla" in American schools reinforced familiar findings and added insights from a number of new and more recent efforts to untangle the role of genetics and environment as correlates of educational attainment and learning.[40] There are, indeed, literally mountains of data showing a relationship between socioeconomic status and achievement, and Berliner's talk came as a much-needed reminder in an age where most of the policy action is aimed at holding schools and teachers accountable for the success of students—with insufficient attention to the gorilla.

Following my suggestion that the first step involves situating a research project in terms of its general characteristics, I would argue that Berliner's broad analysis of achievement and poverty clearly falls in the category of description: it is about patterns in large and complex data but not intendedly about the effects of a specific treatment on a specific outcome. It is perhaps an example of social evaluation but certainly not program evaluation. (N.B.: It is clear that knowledge about the interactions of economic status and educational progress, which have been accumulating at least since the famous Coleman study of the 1960s, have mostly not been based on randomized experiments.) In short, there is no question about the significance of this type of research for the purpose of elucidating broad relationships and building awareness of the complexities surrounding education reforms.

My concern, however, is that inferences may be drawn from Berliner's analysis that exceed its own evidentiary limits. I do not have empirical evidence, but I would surmise that many people who heard his lecture left the room thinking that poverty *causes* low achievement, and some may have even inferred that until poverty is eradicated it is futile to invest in education reforms. There was scant mention in the lecture of the evidence that investments in education are correlated positively with future labor market outcomes—that is, that the implicit causal relation between poverty and schooling may go in both directions. Knowing David, I know he does not believe that poverty necessarily causes educational failure (he himself did not grow up rich and is about as well educated as our society allows). And I am certain he would be deeply troubled by the inference that spending on schools is futile in the light of the overwhelming constraints imposed by socioeconomic status of students. These are reasons to worry about the perhaps inevitable leap from a rich and nuanced description to a questionable set of policy inferences.

My humble recommendation, therefore, is that it is simply not enough to repeat the tiresome notion that "correlation does not imply causality," which David (and most of the people hearing his lecture and reading it in print) know full well. It is, rather, incumbent on the researcher to specify clearly the limits of the analysis and to outline explicitly the validity of inferences from the analysis relating to specific policy choices that are otherwise left as an exercise to the listener. This would mean more than including a few caveats at the beginning or end of the paper. Rather, it would involve articulating as precisely as possible the intended and unintended causal inferences embedded in the work; the different standards of evidence that would need to obtain if the results were to translate into policy or programs; cautions about unintended effects of alternate interpretations of the data; and how the discovery of new patterns and reinforcement or refutation of known patterns strengthens the base for testable hypotheses.[41]

Policymakers Should . . .

1. *Curb their political instinct for drama.* It is not surprising to find a certain symmetry between the responsibilities of researchers and policymakers: after all, many policymakers have research training and many researchers crave the real world of policy.[42] In any event, the three recommendations for researchers outlined above have symmetrical analogues for policymakers.

Just as my proposed compact asks researchers to tone down their zeal for methodological purity (number 1), here I propose that policymakers lower their rhetorical and political thermostats. I realize it may be naïve to expect most politicians who want to woo voters to show patience for thoughtful and procedurally rational deliberation toward the definition of reasonable goals and sensible strategies for reaching them. The rhetoric of emergency and rapid progress is terribly compelling.

Nevertheless, it would be worth exploring under what conditions key policymakers might engage with respectable scholars for the sake of coming to mutual agreement over the pace and character of reform initiatives. Given the extent to which all education-policy debates are steeped in ideological conviction, it may be necessary to move the proposed deliberative forum into neutral territory, one in which policy goals are subjected to empirical analysis and empirical results are tested for their broader contextual relevance.[43]

Absent natural incentives among individual politicians to seek reasonable rather than extravagant solutions, a remedy may necessitate some kind of collective action.[44] For example, consider a new reform watchdog group, funded with federal and private money, charged with ranking legislative and other reform proposals on criteria such as intended and unintended consequences, estimated and likely costs, validity of anticipated effects on different population groups, reasonableness of implicit and explicit timelines, etc. The question is whether the establishment of this sort of agency (procedural details pending . . .) might align the incentives of policy-makers, politicians, and researchers and create capacity for long-term reform proposals with procedurally rational features. Will the prospect of published rankings of school-reform initiatives on vari-ous criteria motivate development of procedurally rational propos-als and accountability rules?

2. *Avoid confounding skepticism with apology for the status quo.* Poli-cymakers need to appreciate that scientific research is, by its nature, an exercise in skepticism, and they should not mistake a researcher's penchant for inquiry as apology for the status quo. Scientists (and engineers) are principally motivated by the search for valid descrip-tions and explanations of complex phenomena and solutions that are grounded in theory and experimentation. One of the behaviors that corrodes the value of rigorous inquiry is the propensity for re-jection of research and the ad hominem insinuation that a research-er is politically motivated—just because he or she says that some propositions are flawed or foolish. There is not much to add to this admonition: policymakers should simply assume good and honest intentions by researchers unless there is demonstrable evidence to the contrary.[45]

3. *Promote knowledge accumulation.* The mirror image of the rule that researchers should announce the epistemology and intent of their studies is the requirement that policymakers invite (and sup-port) research that produces different forms of knowledge. Pushing toward a "gold standard" is, in itself, an example of using (or misus-ing) an imaginary fine-tuning knob: the worthy goal is to raise stan-dards of research evidence, but it pays to remember what happens if a thermostat is set too high just because a room feels a little cold. In the quest for more research that is useful for validating claims con-cerning programs or products (e.g., reading curricula), policymak-

ers need to prevent unwanted narrowing of perspectives, remain open to diverse and even confusing information, and reaffirm the value of multidisciplinary and multimethodological studies.

Perhaps most important, policymakers, especially those involved in funding of research, should be wary of defining acceptable evidence too narrowly and setting evidentiary standards too high. The effect of the former is to dismiss scholarship that is outside an accepted epistemology; in the current context, emphasis on the value of randomized trials in estimating causality could be interpreted as a rejection of descriptive, qualitative, observational, and even large-scale econometric studies. As I suggested above (in rule number 3 for researchers), different modalities of research produce different types of findings, useful for different policy and practice decisions; indeed, some research that has no immediately identifiable utility may be the most valuable in terms of generating unanticipated findings and particularly useful innovations.

Setting evidentiary standards too high can have negative unintended effects: the inference that there is insufficient knowledge to justify *any* program or practice. Assume for the sake of argument that most methodological purists have good intentions: the application of rigorous scientific inquiry to inform (if not to solve) complex policy problems. Then the possibility that more and more rigor will lead to less and less interest in research by decisionmakers should give pause. The alternative to such methodological purity is the awareness that decisions will have to be made and that some formal knowledge—even if it is incomplete—should be viewed favorably, whereas the resistance to making decisions until complete, final, and definitive evidence has been acquired would be foolish and damaging to prospects for genuine school improvement.

A FINAL WORD

This book, and the proposed compact aimed at better coexistence among researchers and users of research, is a plea for rationality in the organization, production, and utilization of knowledge for education policy and reform. The pursuit of better research, better policy, and better practice requires experimentation, trial and error, learning-by-doing, patience, and improved mutual respect. Above all, it requires acceptance of the possibility that it makes more sense to seek better solutions than to wait for the best.

Notes

INTRODUCTION

1. See, e.g., Aaron Beck, *Cognitive Therapy and the Emotional Disorders* (New York: Meridian, 1976).
2. "Traveling Salesman Problem," available online at *http://www.tsp.gatech.edu.*
3. It seems that the minimalist criterion for "computationally feasible" is that the result be attainable in one's lifetime.
4. The debate over face validity of economic assumptions is relevant, indeed partially motivated by these concerns, but would take us on a long and winding tangential road here. Interested readers are encouraged to study the arguments in Richard Cyert and James G. March, *A Behavioral Theory of the Firm* (Cambridge, MA: Blackwell Business, 1992). One student of rationality in economic theory suggests its biblical roots: "In models of full rationality, all relevant information is assumed to be available to *homo economicus* at no cost. This classical version . . . has a distinctive Christian flavor: he is created in the image of an omniscient God." See Gert Gigerenzer, "Striking a Blow for Sanity in Theories of Rationality," in *Models of a Man: Essays in Memory of Herbert A. Simon*, ed. Mies Augier and James G. March (Cambridge, MA: MIT Press, 2004), 389–410.
5. The term *bounded rationality* has become a staple of economics and psychology (and their intersection). See, e.g., Herbert A. Simon, "Bounded Rationality," in *The New Palgrave: A Dictionary of Economics,* ed. John Eatwell, Murray Milgate, and Peter Newman (New York: W. W. Norton, 1990).
6. Even the most mathematically proficient economists acknowledge the limits of formal, structured, algorithm-driven decisions, especially in stressful times. Commenting on the nomination of Ben Bernanke as chairman of the

Federal Reserve, economist David Romer offered that Mr. Bernanke would be judicious in his reliance on models. "He of course understands that even in normal times, the best model is just a guide . . . if something extraordinary happens, like either Russia goes under or the stock market goes down by 20 percent, anyone with a modicum of common sense knows that the model's not going to be a reliable guide." Daniel Altman, "Bernanke Models, and Their Limits," *New York Times,* October 30, 2005, pp. B4–6. To the extent that Bernanke's predecessor, Alan Greenspan, achieved almost God-like status despite his preference for large doses of intuitive judgment to balance formal econometric forecasts, my friend R was obviously in very good company.

7. There is an intriguing symmetry here that deserves the attention of historians of science. Computer science, which has enabled development of algorithms to solve even large-sized TSPs, was strongly influenced by research on human cognition, while modern theories of cognition have been strongly influenced by the advent of electronic computing. Not surprisingly, Simon was a major force stimulating this convergence. I discuss this again later.

8. Herbert A. Simon, "From Substantive to Procedural Rationality," in *Method and Appraisal in Economics*, ed. Spiro J. Latsis (Cambridge, Eng.: Cambridge University Press, 1976), 65–86. See also Herbert A. Simon, "Rationality as Process and as Product of Thought," *American Economic Review* 68 (1978): 1–16.

9. William James "ended up inventing a philosophy, pragmatism, that is supposed to enable people to make *good* choices among philosophical options . . . [and] believed that a risk-assuming decisiveness—betting on an alternative even before all the evidence is in—was the supreme mark of character." Louis Menand, *The Metaphysical Club* (New York: Farrar, Straus & Giroux, 2001), 75 (italics added).

10. For the best explanation of positivism in economics, see Milton Friedman, "The Methodology of Positive Economics," in *Essays in Positive Economics* (Chicago: University of Chicago Press, 1953).

11. Simon, "From Substantive to Procedural Rationality," 65.

12. See, e.g., Oliver E. Williamson, *Markets and Hierarchies: Analysis and Antitrust Implications* (New York: Free Press, 1975); Jennifer Halpern and Robert Stern, eds., *Debating Rationality: Aspects of Organizational Decision-Making* (Ithaca, NY: Cornell University Press, 1998).

13. Noteworthy attempts to introduce these concepts to the debate over education policy, which are theoretically compelling but sadly underutilized,

are found in just a few articles: see Richard Murnane and Richard Nelson, "Production and Innovation When Techniques Are Tacit: The Case of Education," *Journal of Economic Behavior and Organization* 5 (September–December 1984): 353–73; Ernest House, "A Framework for Appraising Educational Reforms," *Educational Researcher* 25, no. 7 (1996): 6–14; and Brian Rowan and Cecil Miskel, "Institutional Theory and the Study of Educational Organizations," in *Handbook of Research on Educational Administration*, ed. Joseph Murphy and Karen S. Louis (San Francisco: Jossey-Bass, 1999).

CHAPTER I. COGNITIVE SCIENCE, LEARNING, AND ORGANIZATION

1. For one of the more accessible reviews of this burgeoning science, I recommend Howard Gardner, *The Mind's New Science: A History of the Cognitive Revolution* (New York: Basic, 1985).

2. Simon summarized cognitive psychology's contribution to learning this way: "Learning research is concerned with the way in which information is extracted from one problem situation and stored in such a way as to facilitate the solving of similar problems subsequently. Problem solving research . . . focuses especially upon the complementary roles of trial-and-error procedures and insight in reaching problem solutions." Herbert A. Simon, "From Substantive to Procedural Rationality," in *Method and Appraisal in Economics*, ed. Spiro J. Latsis (Cambridge, Eng.: Cambridge University Press, 1976), 129–48.

3. Ellen Condliffe Lagemann, *An Elusive Science: The Troubling History of Education Research* (Chicago: University of Chicago Press, 2000).

4. See Gardner, *Mind's New Science.*

5. For positivism in economics, the classic defense is Milton Friedman, "The Methodology of Positive Economics," in *Essays in Positive Economics* (Chicago: University of Chicago Press, 1953).

6. Lagemann, *Elusive Science*, 214.

7. MANIAC stood for Mathematical Analyzer, Numerical Integrator and Computer. See Lagemann, *Elusive Science*, 214. For a brief history of ENIAC, see *http://ftp.arl.mil/~mike/comphist/eniac-story.html.*

8. For evidence of the awareness of this strange and wonderful convergence on the part of some of the early giants in the field, see Gardner, *Mind's New Science*, 28ff. Ulric Neisser's *Cognitive Psychology* (New York: Appleton-Century-

Crofts, 1967) was one of the first and most influential texts for this new science. Miller and Simon were critical players in the arena in which emerging computer theory converged with evolving learning and thinking theory. They were both instrumental in the development of new approaches to understanding and improving human problem solving, but Simon soon took this science in the direction of social interactions and organization theory as well.

9. For additional information about the underpinnings of cognitive theory, see, e.g., James Greeno, Alan Collins, and Lauren Resnick, "Cognition and Learning," in *Handbook of Educational Psychology*, ed. David Berliner and Robert Calfee (New York: Macmillan, 1996).

10. Howard Gardner, *Frames of Mind: The Theory of Multiple Intelligences* (New York: Basic, 1983), 22ff. See also Lee Shulman and Neil Carey, "Psychology and the Limitations of Individual Rationality: Implications for the Study of Reasoning and Civility," *Review of Educational Research* 54, no. 4 (Winter 1984): 501–24. The authors note one of the ironies in the relation between psychology and education: "Precisely at the time when the influence of the rational model was waning in psychology, to be replaced by the perspective of bounded rationality, the scientific study of teaching began to flourish . . . and it was clearly the rational view of behavioral functionalism" (506).

11. Lauren Resnick, *Education and Learning to Think* (Washington, DC: National Academy Press, 1987). Available at *http://www.nap.edu/books/0309037859/html/index.html*

12. See, e.g., Edward L. Thorndike, *The Principles of Teaching Based on Psychology* (New York: Seiler, 1916).

13. See also J. Greeno, "Some Examples of Cognitive Task Analysis with Instructional Applications," in *Aptitude, Learning, and Instruction,* ed. Richard E. Snow and Marshall J. Farr (Hillsdale, NJ: Lawrence Erlbaum, 1980). For a decision-theoretic approach to learning theory that blends cognitive principles with notions of optimal pedagogical strategy, see Richard C. Atkinson, "Ingredients for a Theory of Instruction," *American Psychologist* 22, no. 1 (October 1972): 921–931.

14. Resnick's visualization of content and performance standards in education, though spurred by the post–*A Nation at Risk* zeitgeist, called for a much more cognitively inspired pedagogy than had been anticipated by the framers of that incredibly influential report. This is just one of the ironies of the reform movement of the last 20 years.

15. See, e.g., Kurt W. Fischer and M. H. Immordino-Yang, "Cognitive Development and Education: From Dynamic General Structure to Specific

Learning and Teaching," in *Traditions of Scholarship in Education*, ed. Ellen Condliffe Lagemann (Chicago: Spencer Foundation, 2002). For a summary and explanation of how rival models of human rationality affected learning theory, see Shulman and Carey, "Psychology and the Limitations of Individual Rationality."

16. For a good overview of the assessment controversies of the 1980s, see U.S. Congress, Office of Technology Assessment, *Asking the Right Questions: Testing in American Schools* (Washington, DC: Government Printing Office, 1992).

17. See, e.g., National Research Council, *Transitions in Work and Learning: Implications for Assessment*, ed. Alan Lesgold (Washington, DC: National Academy Press, 1997); and National Research Council, *Enhancing Human Performance: Issues, Theories, and Techniques*, ed. Daniel Druckman and John A. Swets (Washington, DC: National Academy Press, 1988); Ethel Tobach et al., eds., *Mind and Social Practice: Selected Writings of Sylvia Scribner* (Cambridge, Eng.: Cambridge University Press, 1997); R. Sternberg, *Beyond IQ: A Triarchic Theory of Human Intelligence* (New York: Cambridge University Press, 1985); Howard Gardner, *Multiple Intelligence: The Theory in Practice* (New York: Basic, 1993); John Anderson, Lynn Reder, and Herbert A. Simon, "Situated versus Cognitive Perspectives: Form versus Substance," *Educational Researcher* 26, no. 1 (1997): 18–21. The work of Robert Glaser and colleagues (including Resnick) at the University of Pittsburgh's Learning Research and Development Center has influenced a generation of education researchers. See, e.g., Robert Glaser, "Cognitive Science and Education," *International Social Science Journal* 40, no. 1 (February 1988): 21–44.

18. This section draws from National Research Council, *How People Learn: Brain, Mind, Experience, and School*, ed. John D. Bransford, Ann L. Brown, and Rodney R. Cocking (Washington, DC: National Academy Press, 1999).

19. For a glimpse into the debate over situativity and transfer, see, e.g., Anderson et al., "Situated versus Cognitive Perspectives."

20. Recent work on the cognitive-developmental aspects of science teaching and learning continues in this tradition. See, e.g., Katherine E. Metz, "On the Complex Relation between Cognitive Developmental Research and Children's Science Curricula," *Review of Educational Research* 67, no. 1 (1997): 151–63.

21. This section draws from National Research Council, *Knowing What Students Know: The Science and Design of Educational Assessment*, ed. James Pel-

legrino, Naomi Chudowsky, and Robert Glaser (Washington, DC: National Academy Press, 2001). The committee's rationale was captured succinctly by Robert Mislevy, a member of the committee: "It is only a slight exaggeration to describe the test theory that dominates educational measurement today as the application of 20th century statistics to 19th century psychology." See Robert Mislevy, "Foundations of a New Test Theory," in *Test Theory for a New Generation of Tests*, ed. Norman Frederickson, Robert Mislevy, and Isaac I. Bejar (Hillsdale, NJ: Lawrence Erlbaum, 1993).

22. Oliver E. Williamson, *Markets and Hierarchies: Analysis and Antitrust Implications* (New York: Free Press, 1975); and Oliver E. Williamson, *The Economic Institutions of Capitalism: Firms, Markets, and Relational Contracting* (New York: Free Press, 1985).

23. The best treatment of mutually accepted coercion is in Mancur Olson's short and brilliant book, *The Logic of Collective Action: Public Goods and the Theory of Groups* (New York: Schocken, 1968).

24. For a political formulation of the problem, see, e.g., Charles Lindblom, *Politics and Markets: The World's Political Economic Systems* (New York: Basic, 1977); for a sociological perspective, see W. Richard Scott, *Organizations: Rational, Natural, and Open Systems* (Englewood Cliffs, NJ: Prentice Hall, 1981).

25. Williamson notes that his starting-off point, that "markets are ubiquitous," is a convenience and that organizational failure applies equally to markets and firms. See Williamson, *Markets and Hierarchies*, 20.

26. Herbert A. Simon, *Models of Man* (New York: John Wiley and Sons, 1957), 199. The connections between bounded rationality and organization are at the core of the classic work by James March and Herbert A. Simon, *Organizations* (New York: John Wiley and Sons, 1958).

27. Williamson, *Markets and Hierarchies*, 20.

28. See also recent work by Michael Kearns, e.g., "Convergence of Social Science and Computer Science . . . and How It Can Inform Policy," Henry and Bryna David Lecture, Division of Behavioral and Social Sciences and Education, National Research Council, November 9, 2004.

29. Williamson, *Markets and Hierarchies*, 24.

30. Williamson, *Markets and Hierarchies*, 25. Note, again, the connection between this statement and my characterization of how the rational salesman solves his route-selection problem.

31. Williamson, *Markets and Hierarchies*, 25. See also March and Simon, *Organizations*, 161ff.

32. Williamson, *Markets and Hierarchies*, 25.

33. John S. Carroll, John Sterman, and A. Marcus, "Playing the Maintenance Game: How Mental Models Drive Organizational Decision," in *Debating Rationality: Non-Rational Elements of Organizational Decision Making*, ed. Jennifer J. Halpern and Robert N. Stern (Ithaca, NY: Cornell University Press), 99–121.

34. Carroll et al., "Playing the Maintenance Game," 119–20.

35. Carroll et al., "Playing the Maintenance Game," 120.

36. See Colin Camerer, "Behavioral Economics and Nonrational Organizational Decision Making," in *Debating Rationality*, ed. Jennifer Halpern and Robert Stern (Ithaca, NY: Cornell University Press), 53–77.

37. Gary Becker, *Human Capital: A Theoretical and Empirical Analysis, with Special Reference to Education*, 2nd ed. (New York: National Bureau of Economic Research / Columbia University Press, 1975).

38. In France, for example, a law passed in 1972 required firms with more than a certain number of employees to set aside a portion of their budgets for "formation permanente," which led quickly to the sprouting of all kinds of schools offering everything from language to computer training. Whether the return on this large public investment has been realized is, of course, a complicated matter. As a young college graduate in Paris in 1974, however, I found work explaining American idiomatic English to Parisian office workers during their lunch hours and can attest that, thanks to enlightened French labor policy, there are today more Parisians who know the difference between hot dogs and hot rods.

39. Lawrence Cremin, *Popular Education and Its Discontents* (New York: Harper and Row, 1990), 58–59. Nell Eurich's *Corporate Classrooms: The Learning Business* (Princeton, NJ: Carnegie Foundation for the Advancement of Teaching, 1985) was a catalyst for new economic analyses of the so-called "third sector" of firm-provided education and training.

40. See, e.g., Michael Feuer, Henry Glick, and Anand Desai, "Is Firm-Sponsored Education Viable?" *Journal of Economic Behavior and Organization* 8 (Spring 1987): 121–36.

41. Other areas in which this approach has made important inroads include "vertical integration" and antitrust (Williamson, *Markets and Hierarchies*); employment (Oliver E. Williamson, Michael Wachter, and Jeffrey Harris, "Understanding the Employment Relation: The Analysis of Idiosyncratic Exchange," *Bell Journal of Economics* 6 [Spring 1975]: 250–78); production in regulated industries (Scott Masten, "The Organization of Production: Ev-

idence from the Aerospace Industry, *Journal of Law and Economics* 27 [October 1984]: 403–17; Thomas Palay, "Comparative Institutional Economics: The Governance of Rail Freight Contracting," *Journal of Legal Studies* 13 [June 1984]: 265–87); and management decisionmaking to avert disaster (Howard Kunreuther and Jacqueline Meszaros, "Organizational Choice under Ambiguity: Decision Making in the Chemical Industry Following Bhopal," in *Organizational Decision Making*, ed. Zur Shapira [Cambridge, Eng.: Cambridge University Press, 1997], 61–80).

42. Almost until his death, Simon continued to debate his colleagues in economics and psychology who adhered to their own views of rationality and its uses in positive science. William Baumol reports on a debate he witnessed between Simon and Milton Friedman (date unspecified, although presumably within the decade prior to Simon's death): "The subject was the role of rational calculation in economic decisions, Milton arguing the rationality of the optimization premise and Herb defending the reality and reasonableness of *satisficing*." See William J. Baumol, "On Rational Satisficing," in *Models of a Man: Essays in Memory of Herbert A. Simon*, ed. Mies Augier and James March (Cambridge, MA: MIT Press, 2004), 58 (italics added). *Satisficing* is the term Simon conjured to describe how people find "solutions that are good enough for their purposes but that they can obtain with the limited cognitive resources they have available" (Pat Langley, "Heuristics for Scientific Discovery," in *Models of a Man*, 467).

CHAPTER 2. COMPLEXITY BY DESIGN

1. I paraphrase the minister's remarks from my recollection of the meeting; there was no written transcript. For more about the origins and status of French innovations in science teaching, influenced largely by scientists Yves Quere, Pierre Lena, and Georges Charpak in France and Leon Lederman in the United States, see *http://www.inrp.fr/lamap* (accessed February 18, 2005). For a gripping account of Allègre's political rise and fall, see his *Toute verité est bonne à dire* (Paris: Robert Laffont, 2000). I should add a caveat: Allègre's characterization of the degree of central control, as well as the often-heard quip that "if it's Tuesday, all French 4th graders are reading the same page at the same time," are probably more mythic than real. I am grateful to Dan Resnick for his observation that "the French have given us the prototypical state model of a centralized and meritocratic educational system, with little choice or participation, but that system has been refash-

ioned considerably since the breakdown and alienation registered in 1968" (personal communication, February 2005).

2. This is to the often bitter chagrin of Marxists and other ideologically driven opponents of capitalism. For analysis of capitalism's self-preserving mechanisms, see, e.g., Joseph Schumpeter, *Capitalism, Socialism, and Democracy* (New York: Harper and Brothers, 1950); and Oliver E. Williamson, *The Economic Institutions of Capitalism: Firms, Markets, and Relational Contracting* (New York: Free Press, 1985).

3. Here is Adam Smith's original formulation of this extraordinary metaphor: every individual "intends only his own security; and by directing that industry in such a manner as its produce may be of the greatest value, he intends only his own gain, and he is in this, as in many other cases, led by an invisible hand to promote an end which was no part of his intention." Adam Smith, *An Inquiry into the Nature and Causes of the Wealth of Nations*, ed. Edwin Cannan (Chicago: University of Chicago Press, 1976), 1:477. Williamson adopts this general stance; that is, he assumes that "in the beginning there were markets" but hastens to clarify that ultimately his model treats the markets and bureaucracy choice problem symmetrically. See Oliver E. Williamson, *Markets and Hierarchies: Analysis and Antitrust Implications* (New York: Free Press, 1975), 20.

4. For the classic statement, see Gary S. Becker, *Human Capital: A Theoretical and Empirical Analysis*, 2nd ed. (Chicago: University of Chicago Press, 1975). As for taxation, I include property taxation, the preferred American mechanism for raising public funds to support education. Even Social Security, one of the more sacred institutions of America's unique approach to modulated capitalism, is a target for revision after only 70 years; public education in the United States has already lasted twice that long. For evidence of American public opinion on education see, e.g., *http://www.pdkintl.org/kappan/k0409pol.htm* (accessed February 18, 2005).

5. For recent trends, see *http://nces.ed.gov/programs/coe/2004/section1/table.asp?tableID=37* (accessed February 18, 2005).

6. See, e.g., *http://www.aft.org/presscenter/releases/2002/071702.htm* (accessed February 18, 2005) and *http://www.ed.gov/rschstat/eval/choice/pcsp-final/execsum.html* (accessed February 18, 2005).

7. Opponents of school choice are likely to bristle at my suggestion that No Child Left Behind represents a middle-ground solution. To understand my intent here, I recommend placing more emphasis on the word "public" than on the word "choice."

8. Economists may recognize here traces of "revealed preference theory," which posits that observed outcomes are at least implicitly the result of free choice from a given range of options. This reasoning would be hopelessly tautological were it not for the fact that economic theory is by no means silent on the counterfactual possibility. A rich literature is devoted to consideration of circumstances in which observed phenomena (including how various economic and social transactions are organized) reflect a distortion in the way individual preferences are aggregated into systemic outcomes. See, e.g., Kenneth J. Arrow, *Social Choice and Individual Values* (New York: Wiley, 1951); Amartya K. Sen, *Collective Choice and Social Welfare* (San Francisco: Holden-Day, 1970); and Thomas Schelling, *Micromotives and Macrobehavior* (New York: Norton, 1978).

9. The counterfactual reinforces the point. Suppose there was evidence of widespread preference for some alternative, for example, privatization and vouchers; it would be difficult to argue that under such circumstances the survival of the public system should be called "rational." Rather, the literature on distortions between individual preferences and social outcomes would be germane. Without compelling evidence that the nation has been saddled with an unwanted system due to fundamental flaws in the aggregation of citizens' preferences, calling the system "rational" is not without merit.

10. In a recent presentation to the National Research Council governing board, Lee Shulman argued convincingly that even apparently simple instructional tasks, like teaching two-digit multiplication, are cognitively as complex as the most complicated diagnostic and treatment decisions faced by physicians in emergency rooms. See his *The Wisdom of Practice: Essays on Teaching, Learning, and Learning to Teach*, ed. Suzanne M. Wilson (San Francisco: Jossey-Bass, 2004), for elaboration of this theme.

11. The phrase *procedural rationality* is explained in a seminal paper by Herbert A. Simon, "From Substantive to Procedural Rationality," in *Method and Appraisal in Economics,* ed. Spiro J. Latsis (Cambridge, Eng.: Cambridge University Press, 1976), 129–48.

12. Of course, some hyperbole may actually be necessary and good for reform. Perhaps the best example of rhetoric that raced ahead of empirical validity was the brilliant *A Nation at Risk* (Washington, DC: Government Printing Office, 1983). A close second, in terms of dramatic overpromising, is the requirement in the No Child Left Behind Act that all American students reach proficiency in reading and mathematics in 12 years. See, e.g., Robert

Linn, "Accountability: Responsibility and Reasonable Expectations," *Educational Researcher* 32, no. 7 (October 2003).

13. The question arises: Is procedural rationality a positive model of how human beings think, a normative model aimed at prescribing remedial steps toward more rational judgment, or some combination? As Herb Simon once quipped, "A normative model becomes positive if enough people follow the norms," and so I am inclined to finesse this question and leave the reader to sort out the epistemological subtleties.

14. As reported in David B. Tyack, *The One Best System: A History of American Urban Education* (Cambridge, MA: Harvard University Press, 1974). Cited also in U.S. Congress, Office of Technology Assessment, *Testing in American Schools: Asking the Right Questions* (Washington, DC: Government Printing Office, 1992). NAEP is the National Assessment of Educational Progress, a program initiated in the late 1960s to provide broad national and regional indicators of educational performance; PISA is the Program for International Student Assessment, sponsored by the Organization for Economic Cooperation and Development; and TIMSS is the Trends in International Mathematics and Science Study, one of the most influential reports comparing international educational achievement.

15. See, e.g., Banesh Hoffman, *The Tyranny of Testing* (New York: Crowell-Collier, 1962); and Nicholas Lemann, *The Big Test: The Secret History of the American Meritocracy* (New York: Farrar, Straus & Giroux, 1999).

16. The common-school reformers were not always immune from political mischief. In his superb history of urban school reform in America, David Tyack notes how Mann and his colleagues sometimes used tests as "bludgeons of reform." See Tyack, *One Best System*. Testing was not the only irony of the common-school reforms. For an insightful analysis, see Michael Katz, *The Irony of Early School Reform: Educational Innovation in Mid-Nineteenth Century Massachusetts* (Cambridge, MA: Harvard University Press, 1968).

17. A good overview is provided in U.S. Congress, Office of Technology Assessment, *Testing in American Schools*. See also Daniel Resnick, "The History of Educational Testing," in National Research Council, *Ability Testing: Uses, Consequences, and Controversies*, part 2 (Washington, DC: National Academy Press, 1982); and Lee J. Cronbach, "Five Decades of Public Controversy over Mental Testing," *American Psychologist* 30 (January 1975): 1–14. The best history of intelligence testing is Stephen Jay Gould, *The Mismeasure of Man* (New York: Norton, 1996). A recent article that of-

fers another succinct review is Daniel Koretz, "Limitations in the Use of Achievement Tests as Measures of Educators' Productivity," *Journal of Human Resources* 37, no. 4 (2002): 752–77.

18. One should not confound test content with format; even multiple-choice items can measure some higher-order thinking, as the SAT shows. Nevertheless, the only known large-scale testing program (other than those intended for selection and placement in elite educational institutions or specific jobs with higher-order performance requirements) that invests significant resources in the definition and measurement of more complex aspects of learning is the National Assessment of Educational Progress, but its design is fundamentally different from tests that provide individual-level scores. See National Research Council, *Grading the Nation's Report Card: Evaluating NAEP and Transforming the Assessment of Educational Progress* (Washington, DC: National Academy Press, 1999).

19. Daniel Koretz has documented these perverse consequences in a body of research: see, e.g., Koretz, "Limitations in the Use of Achievement Tests as Measures of Educators' Productivity." For an economic model of incentives in testing, see Ed Lazear's very creative "Incentive Issues and Accountability in Education," presentation to the Board on Testing and Assessment, National Research Council, February 2005, *http://www7.nationalacademies. org/BOTA/Lazear_paper.pdf* (accessed February 18, 2005). Lazear's analogy between high-stakes testing and efforts to catch drivers who exceed the speed limit offers an exciting opportunity for broader consideration of performance-based accountability systems. The point, of course, is about the difficulty of devising performance-based accountability systems with accurate fine-tuning dials that raise incentives just enough without causing major unintended distortions. I am reminded in this context of Charles Lindblom's citation of Khrushchev's lament: "It has become the tradition to produce not beautiful chandeliers to adorn homes, but the heaviest chandeliers possible . . . because the heavier the chandeliers produced, the more a factory gets since its output is calculated in tons." See Charles Lindblom, *Politics and Markets* (New York: Basic, 1977), 71. Finally, readers may wish to consider high-stakes testing in the context of research on incentives and effort, as described in chapter 1.

20. This tension came to a head, again, during the debate over voluntary national tests in the late 1990s. For a thorough account of the potentially discriminatory consequences of testing for tracking, promotion, and gradua-

tion decisions, see, e.g., National Research Council, *High Stakes: Testing for Tracking, Promotion, and Graduation* (Washington, DC: National Academy Press, 1999).

21. Some of the better examples of test misuse, such as the infamous wall chart that ranked state education systems by comparing average SAT scores, are described in U.S. Congress, Office of Technology Assessment, *Testing in American Schools*.

22. American Educational Research Association, American Psychological Association, and National Council on Measurement in Education, *Standards for Educational and Psychological Testing* (Washington, DC: American Psychological Association, 1999). Limits to the precision of test scores were well understood by the twentieth-century giants of psychometrics. See, e.g., E. F. Lindquist, "Preliminary Considerations in Objective Test Construction," in *Educational Measurement*, ed. E. F. Lindquist (Washington, DC: American Council on Education, 1951), who emphasized that "the only perfectly valid measure of the attainment of an educational objective would be one based on direct observation of the natural behavior of . . . individuals" (cited in Daniel Koretz, "Score Inflation and Accountability in Education," presentation to the Board on Testing and Assessment, National Research Council, February 2005, *http://www7.nationalacademies.org/BOTA/Koretz_ppt.pdf* [accessed February 18, 2005]). On the importance of designing mechanisms that might be more powerful than codes of conduct and exhortations for appropriate test use, see National Research Council, *High Stakes*.

23. Ed Lazear's presentation on the incentives of testing (*http://www7.national academies.org/BOTA/Lazear_paper.pdf*, accessed February 18, 2005) was motivated in part by a variation on this theme. See also his paper, "Speeding, Tax Fraud, and Teaching to the Test," unpublished manuscript (Hoover Institution and Graduate School of Business, Stanford University, September 2004).

24. Michael J. Feuer, "Linking Tests and Democratic Education," in *Measurement and Research in the Accountability Era*, ed. Carol A. Dwyer (Mahwah, NJ: Lawrence Erlbaum, 2005). This section draws from that paper.

25. The National Assessment of Educational Progress was launched in the mid-1960s when Commissioner of Education Francis Keppel concluded that all the measures floating around the country didn't give him or the public a reliable indication of how students and schools were doing. See, e.g., Lyle V. Jones and Ingram Olkin, eds., *The Nation's Report Card: Evolution and Per-*

spectives (Washington, DC: Phi Delta Kappa Education Foundation, 2004); National Research Council, *Grading the Nation's Report Card;* and U.S. Congress, Office of Technology Assessment, *Testing in American Schools.*

26. The joke is attributed to Chester (Checker) Finn, paraphrased here for emphasis.

27. Feuer, "Linking Tests and Democratic Education." It is worth pausing momentarily to consider whether the current manifestation of federal involvement in education, the No Child Left Behind Act, violates this postulate. If so, if indeed we as a nation have crossed the Rubicon and shifted major education authority to the federal government, then historians will have a field day with the rich irony that it happened under a Republican administration rhetorically committed to the shrinking of federal government authority in the lives of Americans.

28. The hostility was palpable, especially for people like Marshall (Mike) Smith, the principal architect of the Clinton plan and a lifetime advocate for school improvement, closing of the achievement gap, and sensible involvement of government in provision of the most important public good, education. More interesting even than this ostensibly partisan dispute is the fact that Goodling's anger was shared by many progressive educators, including some of the most distinguished members of the National Academy of Education. The bipartisan distaste for test-based accountability is worthy of its own historical and political analysis.

29. I have written elsewhere that for the psychometric community, to see the word "linkage" in a federal statute must have felt like an Andy Warhol moment of fleeting fame. See Feuer, "Linking Tests and Democratic Education." The full text of the law and the section on the NRC study is accessible at *http://www.ssa.gov/OP_Home/comp2/F105-078.html* (accessed February 18, 2005).

30. National Research Council, *Uncommon Measures: Equivalence and Linkage Among Educational Tests* (Washington, DC: National Academy Press, 1999).

31. National Research Council, *Uncommon Measures*, 88.

32. National Research Council, *Uncommon Measures*, 88.

33. The pessimism was perhaps not as surprising to those who had grown accustomed to the particularly negative rhetoric emanating from the social sciences more broadly. For an extraordinary indictment of this phenomenon, see Albert Hirschman, *The Rhetoric of Reaction* (Cambridge, MA: Harvard University Press, 1991).

34. National Research Council, *Uncommon Measures*, 4.

35. From the outset, there were those who argued that the NRC committee had adopted an unnecessarily extreme formulation of the charge; some reviewers of the report made the same point. See also Paul W. Holland, "Assessing the Validity of Test Linking: What Has Happened since Uncommon Measures?" in *Measurement and Research in the Accountability Era*, ed. Caroline A. Dwyer (Mahwah, NJ: Lawrence Erlbaum, 2005).

36. Relatively late in his career, Herbert Simon became worried that science had become too preoccupied with *validation* at the expense of *discovery*. If one accepts that scientific inquiry requires a blend of formal knowledge, rules, and intuitive adaptation in the face of uncertainty, then it follows that discovery is itself a rational process—but a procedural one. See, e.g., Herbert A. Simon, Pat Langley, and Gary Bradshaw, "Scientific Discovery as Problem Solving," *Synthese* 47 (1981): 1–27.

37. When a distinguished economist of education was told of plans for a National Research Council study of the quality of education research, he quipped, "Well, finally we'll have a *short* NRC report." See also Carl Kaestle, "The Awful Reputation of Education Research," *Educational Researcher* (January/February 1993): 23.

38. National Research Council, *Preventing Reading Difficulties in Young Children* (Washington, DC: National Academy Press, 1998); National Reading Panel, *Report of the National Reading Panel: Teaching Children to Read* (Washington, DC: National Institute of Child Health and Human Development, 2000).

39. For detailed discussion of the growing interest in evidence from such major reform initiatives as Success for All, see Lisa Towne, "Scientific Evidence and Inference in Educational Policy and Practice: Defining and Implementing 'Scientifically Based' Research," in *Measurement and Research in the Accountability Era*, ed. Caroline A. Dwyer (Mahwah, NJ: Lawrence Erlbaum, 2005).

40. It is important to acknowledge that many educators believed that the entire scientifically based research movement was the invention of conservatives driven to use research to advance their political agenda. Evaluating this claim is clearly beyond the scope of this book.

41. Robert Sweet, as quoted in Margaret Eisenhardt and Lisa Towne, "Contestation and Change in National Policy on 'Scientifically Based' Education Research," *Educational Researcher* 32 (October 2003): 31–38.

42. It is especially interesting to recall the consummate efforts on the part of congressional staff (and members) to write language about quantitative and

qualitative methods. One cannot help suspecting that, faced with a rather thick literature covering arcane epistemological debates, they would have preferred to rewrite the U.S. tax code. For an excellent review and chronology of these efforts, see Eisenhardt and Towne, "Contestation and Change in National Policy on 'Scientifically Based' Education Research."

43. Michael J. Feuer, Lisa Towne, and Richard J. Shavelson, "Scientific Culture and Educational Research," *Educational Researcher* 31, no. 8 (November 2002): 4–14.

44. This phrase is borrowed from Donald E. Stokes, *Pasteur's Quadrant: Basic Science and Technological Innovation* (Washington, DC: Brookings Institution Press, 1997).

45. The committee charged with this massive assignment had all of nine months to deliberate. Were it not for the exquisite teamwork led by committee chair Richard Shavelson and study director Lisa Towne, as well as the existence of a sturdy intellectual infrastructure in the NRC, the timeline for the study would have been deemed not only challenging (which it was) but utterly ridiculous.

46. See Eisenhardt and Towne, "Contestation and Change in National Policy on 'Scientifically Based' Education Research," for a comparison of the law before and after the NRC report.

47. National Research Council, *Scientific Research in Education*, 51.

48. National Research Council, *Scientific Research in Education*, 80.

49. National Research Council, *Scientific Research in Education*, 80, citing Jaren Diamond, *Guns, Germs, and Steel: The Fates of Human Societies* (New York: Norton, 1999).

50. National Research Council, *Scientific Research in Education*, 85.

51. Even the STAR experiment came in for rather strident critiques, perhaps surprisingly from researchers known for their advocacy of scientific method; e.g., Eric A. Hanushek, "Some Findings from an Independent Investigation of the Tennessee STAR Experiment and from Other Investigations of Class Size Effects," *Educational Evaluation and Policy Analysis* 21, no. 2 (1999): 143–64. I am grateful to Lisa Towne for the reminder that although the experiment was hugely influential, it was not considered an unambiguous success.

52. Paul W. Holland, personal communication, 2001.

53. National Research Council, *Scientific Research in Education*, 13–14.

54. I am intrigued by the possibility that the cognitively inspired science of education proposed in this book might have the salutary side benefit of bring-

ing some peace to the warring quantitative and qualitative factions in education research. To see the need for improved relations, the special issue of *Educational Researcher* (November 2002) is a good place to start. See especially Elizabeth A. St. Pierre, "'Science' Rejects Postmodernism." A more recent analysis is in John Willinsky, "Scientific Research in a Democratic Culture: Or What's a Social Science For?" *Teachers College Record* 107, no. 1 (January 2005): 38–51.

CHAPTER 3. TINKERING TOWARD RATIONALITY

1. Larry Cuban and David Tyack, *Tinkering toward Utopia: A Century of Public School Reform* (Cambridge, MA: Harvard University Press, 1996), 10. With gratitude for inspiring the title of this chapter.

2. David Tyack, *The One Best System: A History of American Urban Education* (Cambridge, MA: Harvard University Press, 1974); David Tyack, Robert Lowe, and Elisabeth Hansot, *Public Schools in Hard Times: The Great Depression and Recent Years* (Cambridge, MA: Harvard University Press, 1984); Carl Kaestle, *Pillars of the Republic: Common Schools and American Society, 1780–1860* (New York: Farrar, Straus & Giroux, 1983); Lawrence Cremin, *Popular Education and Its Discontents* (New York: Harper & Row, 1990); David F. Labaree, *The Making of an American High School: The Credentials Market and the Central High School of Philadelphia, 1838–1939* (New Haven, CT: Yale University Press, 1992) and *How to Succeed in School Without Really Learning: The Credentials Race in American Education* (New Haven, CT: Yale University Press, 1997); Michael Katz, *The Irony of Early School Reform: Educational Innovation in Mid-Nineteenth Century Massachusetts* (Cambridge, MA: Harvard University Press, 1968); Ellen Condliffe Lagemann, *An Elusive Science: The Troubling History of Education Research* (Chicago: University of Chicago Press, 2002); Diane Ravitch, *The Great School Wars: A History of the New York City Public Schools* (Baltimore: Johns Hopkins University Press, 2000).

3. I find myself here challenged by the logic of my own argument. If procedural rationality is both a positive and normative framework for studying human decisionmaking, as I suggested in the preceding chapter, then its validity must rest in part on the legitimacy of the assumption that people actually do set reasonable rather than ideal (or utopian) goals, apply appropriate rather than exhaustive (and exhausting) deliberation, and settle for good rather than optimal solutions. Tyack and Cuban's history provides little re-

assurance that the education-policy system in the United States, at least in its grand rhetoric, demonstrates those qualities.

4. I hesitate to open an argument here about causal inference in history, although the question about warrants and their empirical foundations more generally is at the root of current debates over the quality of education research. The issue boils down to this: accurate and objective *descriptions* of complex phenomena are necessary but not sufficient as a basis for *explaining* those phenomena. Thus, for example, my only quarrel with Diane Ravitch's superb review of the politics and history of textbooks, *The Language Police* (New York: Knopf, 2003), is that it lacks an explanatory model that might link description to policy. It is not necessarily the historian's burden to provide such a model but rather up to the policy-analysis community to build from the good historiography and look for appropriate explanatory and predictive theories.

5. My good friend Bob Hauser has quipped that my preoccupation with the fragility of human thought and action reminds him of the late pope's rejection of the Enlightenment and its hopes for human perfectibility. I guess this is what friends are for . . . but I know Bob well enough to appreciate that behind such friendly jabs lie profound questions that shouldn't be ignored.

6. The reference is to the recent best seller by Malcolm Gladwell, *Blink: The Power of Thinking without Thinking* (Boston: Little, Brown, 2005).

7. The combination of disappointment with inconclusive results and the often obscure jargon in which social research is couched can have a devastating effect on public support. Senator William Proxmire's Golden Fleece Awards in the 1970s and President Reagan's draconian cuts to social-research budgets in the 1980s are two relatively recent reminders.

8. Albert Hirschman, *The Rhetoric of Reaction* (Cambridge, MA: Harvard University Press, 1991). Hirschman is an economist and economic historian par excellence, but, like other historians, he *describes* a phenomenon but stops short of providing a compelling explanatory theory. Here he alerts his readers to a fundamental threat to democratic discourse, but without further explanation of the roots of the behavior he chronicles (the assertion that any given program will have perverse consequences, jeopardize other programs or policies, or have no effect at all), it is unlikely that his legitimate call for a remedy will be heeded. His description of the long tradition in the social sciences to highlight (sometimes gleefully) unintended negative consequences of social action is riveting, but it begs an explanatory theory. My

choice would be to start with cognitive psychology—that is, with the hypothesis that the rhetoric of perversity, jeopardy, and futility might be explained in terms of some combination of bounded rationality, risk aversion, and self-interest seeking on the part of scholars and commentators. I save the unpacking of this hypothesis for a later paper. Meanwhile, I commend to readers interested in the pervasiveness of this mentality in modern political discourse a recent article by Martin Peretz, "The Politics of Churlishness," *New Republic*, April 11, 2005. The term *methodological nihilism* was coined by an anonymous reviewer of a recent NRC report.

9. I am indebted to Mike McPherson for his help in sorting out these issues. I quote and paraphrase here from personal communications with him, with apologies for any misrepresentation and deep gratitude for his thoughtfulness.

10. John Rawls, *A Theory of Justice* (Cambridge, MA: Belknap Press of Harvard University Press, 1971).

11. Cremin, *Popular Education*, 85.

12. For a lively discussion of alternate ways of understanding bounded and procedural rationality, see several of the chapters in *Models of a Man: Essays in Memory of Herbert A. Simon*, ed. Mies Augier and James March (Cambridge, MA: MIT Press, 2004), especially Kenneth Arrow, "Is Bounded Rationality Unboundedly Rational? Some Ruminations"; William Baumol, "On Rational Satisficing"; and Gerd Gigerenzer, "Striking a Blow for Sanity in Theories of Rationality."

13. As suggested in chapter 1, the seminal work that builds on concepts of bounded rationality and complexity for a new institutional economics and establishes a foundation for a behavioral theory of organizations is Oliver E. Williamson's *Markets and Hierarchies: Analysis and Antitrust Implications* (New York: Free Press, 1975) and *The Economic Institutions of Capitalism* (New York: Free Press, 1985). Two efforts that explore implications of aspects of the Williamson model for education are Richard Murnane and Richard Nelson, "Production and Innovation When Techniques Are Tacit: The Case of Education," *Journal of Economic Behavior and Organization* 5 (1984): 353–73; and Ernest House, "A Framework for Appraising Educational Reforms," *Educational Researcher* 25, no. 7 (October 1996): 6–14.

14. Sharon Begley, *Wall Street Journal*, December 10, 2004.

15. I am hinting here at the difference between knowing, which implies certainty, and know-how, which captures the more complex dependence of rational judgment on experience, intuition, and formal knowledge. Richard

Nelson's attention to know-how in the context of innovation and economic development generally, and education specifically, has helped my thinking. See, for example, Richard R. Nelson, "On the Nature and Evolution of Human Know-How," *Research Policy* 31 (2002): 719–33.

16. It is beyond my scope (and expertise) to adjudicate the ongoing debates among philosophers of science about the nature of paradigmatic shifts and other metaphors for knowledge accumulation. For a particularly enjoyable and succinct summary of some of these issues, see Denis Philips and Nicholas Burbules, *Postpositivism and Educational Research* (Lanham, MD: Rowman and Littlefield, 2000). On the issue of scientific discovery as procedural rationality, see my first chapter and, of course, the series of papers by Herbert Simon in which this theory was first advanced: e.g., Herbert A. Simon, "From Substantive to Procedural Rationality," in *Method and Appraisal in Economics*, ed. Spiro J. Latsis (Cambridge, Eng.: Cambridge University Press, 1976), 129–48; "Rationality as Process and as Product of Thought," *American Economic Review* 68, no. 2 (May 1978): 1–16.

17. Two contemporary examples illustrate the importance of this point. Recent efforts to misconstrue the preponderance of evidence concerning evolution as "just a theory" have opened the door to religious interference in scientific thinking and the teaching of science; see, for example, the eloquent arguments by Bruce Alberts and Jay Labov: National Academy of Sciences, *Teaching about Evolution and the Nature of Science* (Washington, DC: National Academy Press, 1998; available online at *http://nap.edu/catalog/5787.html*); National Academy of Sciences, *Science and Creationism: A View from the National Academy of Sciences* (Washington, DC: National Academy Press, 1999; available online at *http://www.nap.edu/catalog/6024.html*); Bruce Alberts and Jay B. Labov, "From the National Academies: Teaching the Science of Evolution," *Cell Biology Education* 3 (Summer 2004): 75–80. On another front, the preponderance of evidence concerning social promotion suggests that the effects of retaining young pupils in grade are more harmful than beneficial; politicians, however, clearly have more than scientific evidence in mind when they announce their intuitively more appealing policies. See, e.g., National Research Council, *High Stakes: Testing for Tracking, Promotion, and Graduation* (Washington, DC: National Academy Press, 1999); Lorrie A. Shepard and Marshall L. Smith, eds., *Flunking Grades: Research and Policies on Retention* (London: Falmer Press, 1989).

18. On positivism in economic science, see Milton Friedman, "The Methodology of Positive Economics," in *Essays in Positive Economics* (Chicago: Univer-

sity of Chicago Press, 1953). The debate between Friedman and the Simon-March-Cyert school is a classic in the literature of the philosophy of social science. See, e.g., Richard Cyert and James March, *A Behavioral Theory of the Firm* (Cambridge, MA: Blackwell Business, 1992).

19. Harvey Leibenstein pioneered the theory of "x-efficiency," which rejected the assumption of technical efficiency. See, e.g., Harvey Leibenstein, "Allocative Efficiency vs. X-Efficiency," *American Economic Review* 56, no. 3 (June 1966): 392–415. More recently, some economists and management scientists (the latter oriented more toward production technology and less focused on positivist prediction) have used "data envelopment" techniques that do not require the assumption of technical efficiency. These models, originally developed in the 1970s, start with the assumption that different producers operate at different distances from the presumed production-possibility frontier. The seminal work in this field is by Abe Charnes, William W. Cooper, and Ed Rhodes, "Measuring the Efficiency of Decision Making Units," *European Journal of Operations Research* 2 (1978): 429–44. Education applications include Anand Desai and Arie Schinnar, "Technical Issues in Measuring Scholastic Achievement Due to Compensatory Education," *Socio-Economic Planning Sciences* 24 (1990): 143–53. See also Leanna Stiefel, Ross Rubenstein, Amy Schwartz, and Jeffrey Zabel, eds., *Measuring School Performance and Efficiency: Implications for Practice and Research*, Yearbook of the American Education Finance Association (Mahwah, NJ: Lawrence Erlbaum Press, 2005).

20. Economic theory is of course more elaborate than this abbreviation would suggest. Nevertheless, the essence is there. Borrowing from the well-known allegory in Jewish literature (in which the great Rabbi Hillel is challenged to explain Judaism while standing on one foot), economic theory can be summarized thus: assume complete information and self-interest by actors in fully competitive markets . . . all the rest is commentary—now go and maximize.

21. Though reminiscent of behaviorism in psychology, with its orientation toward results instead of the processes of complex internal mechanisms, the neoclassical model is quite different from what has come to be known as "behavioral economics." The latter would be more aptly called "cognitive economics," but it's too late to try for that kind of semantic correction. See Cyert and March, *Behavioral Theory;* see also W. Richard Scott, *Organizations: Rational, Natural, and Open Systems*, 5th ed. (Upper Saddle River, NJ: Prentice-Hall, 2002).

22. Economics has been called the dismal science. One wonders how a theory so steeped in positivism could be so fraught with negativity. For a comprehensive explanation of educational-production functions and its most compelling findings, see Eric Hanushek, "The Economics of Schooling: Production and Efficiency in Public Schools," *Journal of Economic Literature* 24, no. 3 (1986): 1141–77.

23. Some advocates of school choice, however, do seem enamored of capitalist production as a model for how the education system should operate. In addition to Friedman's classic and seminal work on vouchers ("The Role of Government in Education," in *Economics and the Public Interest*, ed. Robert Solo [New Brunswick, NJ: Rutgers University Press, 1955]), see Herbert Walberg, *Education and Capitalism: How Overcoming Our Fear of Markets and Economics Can Improve America's Schools* (Palo Alto, CA: Hoover Institution Press, 2003).

24. See the debate between Hanushek and Hedges, Laine, and Greenwald in *Educational Researcher*. Eric A. Hanushek, "The Impact of Differential Expenditures on School Performance," *Educational Researcher* 18, no. 4 (May 1989): 45–51, 62; Larry V. Hedges, R. D. Laine, and R. Greenwald, "Does Money Matter? A Meta-Analysis of Studies of the Effects of Differential School Inputs on Student Outcomes," *Educational Researcher* 23, no. 3 (1994): 5–14; Larry V. Hedges, R. D. Laine, and R. Greenwald, "Money Does Matter Somewhere: A Reply to Hanushek," *Educational Researcher* 23, no. 4 (1994): 9–10. The work of David Cohen, Steve Raudenbush, and Deborah Ball is exemplary of research that uses intensive observation of schools to refine the conventional input-output model. See Deborah Loewenberg Ball, David K. Cohen, and Stephen W. Raudenbush, "Resources, Instruction, and Research," *Education Evaluation and Policy Analysis* 25 (2003): 119–42.

25. Murnane and Nelson, "Production and Innovation." On tacit knowledge see Michael Polanyi, *The Tacit Dimension* (Garden City, NY: Doubleday, 1967). The problem was well understood by Albert Shanker, the famous head of the American Federation of Teachers, who was fond of pointing out, in the context of debates over the content validity of standardized tests, that if one were interested in measuring typing proficiency it would not be sufficient to ask people questions about the placement of the keys in the QWERTY keyboard—one would have to observe them typing.

26. The work of Sylvia Scribner, among others, is noteworthy. See, e.g., Ethel Tobach et al., *Mind and Social Practice: Selected Writings of Sylvia Scribner* (New York: Cambridge University Press, 1997).

27. This should not lead to complete despair. After all, even the Supreme Court could justify a ruling (about pornography) that conceded the impossibility of ex ante definition but affirmed the principle of ex post accountability nevertheless. As Justice Potter Stewart noted, "I shall not today attempt further to define the kinds of material I understand to be embraced within that shorthand description; and perhaps I could never succeed in intelligibly doing so. But I know it when I see it, and the motion picture involved in this case is not that" (*Jacobellis v. Ohio*, 378 U.S. 184, 1964).

28. See, e.g., U.S. Congress, Office of Technology Assessment, *Power On! New Tools for Teaching and Learning*, OTA-SET-379 (Washington, DC: Government Printing Office, 1988). Early theoretical work on computer-assisted instruction was derivative of pioneering modeling by Richard Atkinson, among others, in which pursuit of optimal decisions was an assumed property of learners. See, e.g., Richard C. Atkinson, "Ingredients for a Theory of Instruction," *American Psychologist* 27 (October 1972): 921–31.

29. Murnane and Nelson, "Production and Innovation," 361.

30. Murnane and Nelson, "Production and Innovation," 368.

31. Ernest House, "A Framework for Appraising Educational Reforms," *Educational Researcher* 25, no. 7 (1996): 6–14; and Ernest House and Kenneth Howe, *Values in Evaluation and Social Research* (Thousand Oaks, CA: Sage, 1999).

32. House, "A Framework," 7. See also my discussion of firm-sponsored education and training in chapter 2.

33. See Michael J. Feuer, "Linking Tests and Democratic Education," in *Measurement and Research in the Accountability Era*, ed. Carol A. Dwyer (Mahwah, NJ: Lawrence Erlbaum, in press).

34. Robert Linn's analysis suggesting why the existing goals and timetables of No Child Left Behind are implausible would be a starting point for this rule. See Robert L. Linn, "Accountability: Responsibility and Reasonable Expectations," *Educational Researcher* 32, no. 7 (2003): 3–13.

35. The controversy that erupted over two Rand Corporation reports that seemed to contradict each other is worth revisiting for at least two reasons. First, there is the important substantive issue—namely, the validity of rapid score gains on standardized tests, which my second chapter addresses in the context of the inevitable tensions that arise from the use of tests for high-stakes accountability. Second, germane to the current discussion, it serves as a reminder of the predicament faced by researchers whose pursuit of empirical validity of policy claims is often couched in the kind of rhetoric that

Hirschman (and I) fear can have long-term damaging effects on democratic discourse and the utility of research for policy. See Stephen P. Klein, Laura S. Hamilton, Daniel F. McCaffrey, and Brian M. Stecher, "What Do Test Scores in Texas Tell Us?" (Washington, DC: RAND, October 2000), available at *http://www.rand.org/publications/IP/IP202*; and David W. Grissmer, Ann Flanagan, Jennifer Kawata, and Stephanie Williamson, "Improving Student Achievement: What State NAEP Test Scores Tell Us" (Washington, DC: RAND, October 2000), available at *http://www.rand.org/publications/ MR/MR924*. Also, Jonathan Weisman, "The Texas Education Myth: Only a Test," *New Republic*, April 10, 2000; and my letter to the editor, *New Republic*, April 2000.

36. Hirschman, *Rhetoric of Reaction*, 45.

37. See Susan Saulny, "Higher Student Test Scores Mean Progress? Council Wants Proof," *New York Times*, June 28, 2005; and Michael Winerip, "Test Scores Are Up: So Why Isn't Everybody Cheering?" *New York Times*, June 29, 2005.

38. For precedent, a potentially useful theoretical foundation for the integration of consequences in models of validation is in Sam Messick, "Validity," in *Educational Measurement*, ed. Robert L. Linn, 3rd ed. (New York: American Council on Education, 1989).

39. For an eloquent and succinct discussion, see the unpublished paper by Nancy Cartwright prepared for the National Research Council "think tank" on evidentiary standards in the behavioral and social sciences, April 2005.

40. David Berliner, "Ignoring the Forest, Blaming the Trees: Our Impoverished View of Educational Reform," available online at *http://www.tcrecord.org*.

41. I urge consideration of this suggestion in the context of recommendations of the NRC committee on scientific research in education. See National Research Council, *Advancing Scientific Research in Education* (Washington, DC: National Academy Press, 2004).

42. And then there are those who insist on straddling the fence. But there is no room here for autobiographical catharsis.

43. If the inference here is that policy ideas need to be subjected to scientific scrutiny, but scientists need not concern themselves with the political ramifications of their research, then I have misstated my thesis. Indeed, as I argued earlier, the hubris of scientists who believe in speaking truth to power, as though democratic governance could or should be based solely or even mostly on "objective" research, often interferes with appropriate uses of scientific inquiry in the policy cauldron. As for the establishment of a neutral

institution designed to adjudicate competing claims of researchers, see, e.g., the recent proposal by Lee Shulman, "Seek Simplicity . . . and Distrust It," *Education Week*, June 8, 2005.

44. I am hinting here at a theory to explain the observed tendency toward extreme articulation of educational goals, based loosely on the "commons" metaphor (Garret Hardin, "The Tragedy of the Commons," *Science* 162 [1968]: 1243–48). In essence, individual politicians overstate educational conditions and overpromise reforms in order to maximize (!) political self-interest; the collective result is equivalent to overgrazing in the commons example, i.e., exhaustion of resources and erosion of capacity for meaningful reform. Unpacking this notion is beyond the scope of this chapter.

45. It is worth noting that the propensity toward nasty, personalized attacks against researchers who oppose various policies is not a monopoly held by policymakers. A painful example is the series of postings by advocates of test-based accountability in which some of the most distinguished measurement experts and research organizations are branded "test-bashers." See, e.g., *http://www.educationnews.org/Richard-Phelps-Previous-Columns.htm*.

About the Author

Michael J. Feuer is the executive director of the Division of Behavioral and Social Sciences and Education in the National Research Council (NRC) of the National Academies, where he is responsible for a broad portfolio of studies and other activities aimed at improved economic, social, and education policymaking. He was the first director of the NRC's Center for Education and the founding director of the Board on Testing and Assessment. Before joining the NRC in 1993, Feuer was a senior analyst and project director at the Congressional Office of Technology Assessment. He holds a Ph.D. in Public Policy from the University of Pennsylvania and an MA from the Wharton School, and studied public administration at the Hebrew University of Jerusalem and political science at the Sorbonne. Feuer grew up in New York City, where he attended public school and graduated *cum laude* from Queens College (CUNY) with a major in English literature and journalism. While at Queens he was the campus "stringer" for the *New York Times* and editor of one of the two major student newspapers.

Upon earning his doctorate, Feuer remained at Penn, teaching graduate seminars in education and working at the Higher Education Finance Research Institute, where he specialized in studies of firm-sponsored training. He then joined the faculty of the business school at Drexel University, teaching courses in public policy and management and continuing his research on the economics of human capital.

Feuer was the Burton and Inglis Lecturer at Harvard University in 2004–05; this book is based on those lectures. Feuer's articles and reviews have been published in economics and policy journals, as well as in the *New York Times,* the *Philadelphia Inquirer,* and other newpapers. He was elected to the National Academy of Education in 2003.

Feuer lives in Washington, D.C., with his wife, Dr. Regine B. Feuer, an obstetrician-gynecologist. The Feuers have two grown children.

Index